PRESENTED TO:

FROM:

DEVOTIONS *for* EVERY DAY *of the* YEAR

His PROGRESS
His
PROMISES

The MOST MOVING WORDS EVER WRITTEN
ABOUT *the* PROMISES *of* JESUS

INTEGRITY®
PUBLISHERS

Produced with the assistance of The Livingstone Corporation (www.LivingstoneCorp.com). Introductions written by Neil Wilson. Project staff includes Dave Veerman, Linda Taylor, Ashley Taylor, Kirk Luttrell, Andy Culbertson, Phoebe Blaustein, Don Jones, David Thompson, David Eyk, Nathan White, Terefe Bolteno, Teri Hill, Erika Godfrey, Tom Ristow, Kathy Ristow, and Sara Jones.

Scripture quotations are taken from the following sources:

The Holy Bible, English Standard Version (esv). Copyright © 2001 by Crossway Bibles, a division of Good News Publishers. Used by permission. All rights reserved.

The King James Version (kjv). Public domain.

The New American Standard Bible® (nasb®). Copyright © 1960, 1962, 1963, 1968, 1971, 1972, 1973, 1975, 1977, 1995 by The Lockman Foundation. Used by permission.

The New Century Version® (ncv®). Copyright © 1987, 1988, 1991 by Thomas Nelson, Inc. Used by permission. All rights reserved.

The Holy Bible, New International Version® (niv®). Copyright © 1973, 1978, 1984 by International Bible Society. Used by permission of Zondervan. All rights reserved.

The New King James Version® (nkjv®). Copyright © 1982 by Thomas Nelson, Inc. Used by permission. All rights reserved.

The Holy Bible, New Living Translation® (nlt®). Copyright © 1996. Used by permission of Tyndale House Publishers, Inc., Wheaton, Illinois 60189. All rights reserved.

The New Revised Standard Version® (nrsv®). Copyright © 1989, 1995 by the Division of Christian Education of the National Council of the Churches of Christ in the United States of America. Used by permission. All rights reserved.

Cover and Interior Design: Brand Navigation, LLC. www.brandnavigation.com

Cover and Interior Images: Pixelworks Studio, Steve Gardner

ISBN 1-59145-272-4

Printed in China

05   06   07   08   09 RRD 10 9 8 7 6 5 4 3 2 1

TABLE OF CONTENTS

INTRODUCTION

Promises saturate life. We move and breathe because of promises, many of which we don't really think about. Cars we drive, chairs that support us, medicines we take—all these depend in part on the ability and willingness of people to make promises. Perhaps our capacity for promises is one of the overlooked traits that demonstrate we are made in the image of God.

God is the ultimate promise maker and keeper. We promise, but prove ourselves often unable or unwilling to keep our promises. God demonstrates Himself both able and willing. A person's word is his bond within human limitation; God's word establishes an absolute bond. God does what He says He will do. Revel in His promises as you sample their wonders in the pages that follow.

WHY
PROMISES?

For no matter how many promises
God has made, they are "Yes" in Christ.
And so through him the "Amen" is
spoken by us to the glory of God.

2 CORINTHIANS 1:20 NIV

WHY PROMISES?

A relationship cannot exist, much less progress, without promises. We owe our very lives to promises kept. The quality of marriage vows and parental promises creates the conditions that lead to our birth and upbringing. We are the products of promises.

As much as we value the impact of promises, their importance grows as we realize how much our relationship with God is based on promises. When we begin to look for them, God's specific commitments overwhelm us.

This section examines the impact of promises on our lives and the importance they have for our understanding of God's character. God's promises and His faithfulness to them become one of the primary vehicles by which we come to know God personally. Ultimately, our exercise of faith and trust requires that we take one or more of God's promises at face value and make it a reason for decisions or choices we make.

BREAKING SIN'S POWER

COLOSSIANS 1:4–5 NLT

*We have heard that you trust in Christ Jesus and
that you love all of God's people. You do this because
you are looking forward to the joys of heaven—
as you have been ever since you first heard
the truth of the Good News.*

Sin is what you do when your heart is not satisfied with God. No one sins out of duty. We sin because it holds out some promise of happiness. That promise enslaves us until we believe that God is more to be desired than life itself (Psalm 63:3). Which means that the power of sin's promise is broken by the power of God's. All that God promises to be for us in Jesus stands over against what sin promises to be for us without him. This great prospect of the glory of God is what I call *future grace*. Being satisfied with that is what I call *faith*.

JOHN PIPER

THE ANCHOR OF OUR SOULS

JEREMIAH 17:7 NIV
But blessed is the man who trusts in the LORD,
whose confidence is in him.

In the midst of an ever-changing world, the good news is that the life of faith is anchored by the power, provisions, and promises of God. Circumstances may change, but the future is as sure as the character of God himself. No matter what happens, those who trust in God hope in his word.

The Bible also makes clear that hope in God's promises reveals itself in obedience to his commands, since "every one who . . . hope[s] in him purifies himself, just as he is pure" (1 John 3:3). Those who are "heavenly minded" therefore depart from evil, defend the defenseless, work for justice, pursue peace, give generously, and even love their enemies.

SCOTT HAFEMANN

TRUST AND OBEY

JOHN 14:1 NIV
*"Do not let your hearts be troubled.
Trust in God; trust also in me."*

For every fear we have, God has a promise. There's something about who God is and about what He has promised that meets us at our points of deepest fear. . . . Trust that God is who He says he is. Then step out and obey. Do what God is asking you to do. When you can't figure out how it's all going to work, step out and do it by faith. The more you get to know God, the more you can trust and obey. . . . So we have His promises. We're to be content. We're not to worry about how our future needs will be met. Then when we have a need, rather than fretting or striving or manipulating, what are we to do? Simply ask Him to meet our needs and ask in faith, confident that if He knows this is a need, He will provide it.

NANCY LEIGH DEMOSS

TAKE HOLD OF HOPE

HEBREWS 6:17–18 NIV

*Because God wanted to make the unchanging nature
of his purpose very clear to the heirs of what was
promised, he confirmed it with an oath. God did this
so that . . . we who have fled to take hold of the hope
offered to us may be greatly encouraged.*

Sadly, even a great segment of the church of Jesus
Christ is living far below the level of hope that our
text calls us to! There are many Christians, born-again
believers, who would love to think that there is more to
being saved than just hanging on by our teeth and our
toenails until Jesus returns to bail us out of this mess.
Especially new converts, instead of hearing older Christians take a defeatist attitude, would like to hear a genuine
note of *hope* sounded! William J. Abraham . . . says,
"There is a vast army of new Christians hungry for initi-
ation into a modern version of the Christian faith that
will integrate deep piety, social action, and classical theology in a penetrating expression of the Christian gospel.
A renewed evangelical tradition that holds in tension both
its unity and its diversity can provide exactly this." All the
world would like to hear a genuine word of hope!

RUSSELL METCALFE

PATIENTLY DEPENDING ON GOD'S WORD

ROMANS 15:4 NLT

*Such things were written in the Scriptures long ago
to teach us. They give us hope and encouragement
as we wait patiently for God's promises.*

For whatsoever things were written aforetime. This is an application of his illustration. Paul's purpose is to prevent any of his readers from thinking that his exhortation to imitate Christ was too far-fetched. 'There is nothing,' he says, 'in Scripture which may not contribute to your instruction and the training of your life.'

When he adds *that through patience and through comfort of the scriptures we might have hope,* he does not include the whole of that benefit which is to be derived from the Word of God, but briefly points to its main object. The particular service of the Scriptures is to raise those who are prepared by patience and strengthened by consolation to the hope of eternal life, and to keep their thoughts fixed upon it. . . . The patience of believers is not that hardihood which philosophers enjoin, but the meekness by which we willingly submit to God when the taste of His goodness and fatherly love renders all things sweet to us. This patience cherishes and sustains unceasing hope in us.

JOHN CALVIN

TRUST IN GOD'S WORD

ROMANS 15:4 NIV

For everything that was written in the past was written to teach us, so that through endurance and the encouragement of the Scriptures we might have hope.

Martin Luther reminds us "not in works, not in any other thing, but purely in hope the heart of man rejoices. The one who seeks to find joy apart from this hope will labor much but will labor in vain." Then Luther goes on to remind us of the Bible story of the woman who went from doctor to doctor for twelve years, spending all she had until she met Jesus. . . .

Our hope is not to be found in running from place to place or in smug resignation to the evils of life, but rather in belief and trust in God's word. . . . Thank God for this lamp of truth that burns ever brightly telling us of Jesus of Nazareth, the promised Messiah sent by God to redeem us from the slavery to sin, death, and hopelessness.

JOHN HERRMANN

LED BY THE WORD

PSALM 119:105 NKJV
Your word is a lamp to my feet
And a light to my path.

The Word of God is like a light
That shines serenely thro' the night;
Its rays will light my weary way
To the realms of a fair, unending day.

The Word of God is strong and sure,
Forevermore it shall endure,
When oceans cease to kiss the shore,
When suns shall set to rise no more;
'Mid crash of worlds it shall remain
Unshaken midst the starry rain,
Upon its firm foundation strong,
I will plant my feet thro' the ages long.

HALDOR LILLENAS

FULFILLMENT IN CHRIST

2 CORINTHIANS 1:20 NKJV

*For all the promises of God in Him are Yes, and
in Him Amen, to the glory of God through us.*

All the promises God makes in nature, in Scripture, in
history, and in the longings of personal experience
find their yes in Him. The New Testament speaks of "the
upward call of God in Christ Jesus." Jesus is the upward
call of God—calling us from the lower to the higher, the
incomplete to the complete, the imperfect to the perfect.
Everything in Jesus is upward. Everything outside Jesus is
downward. An African after he was converted renamed
himself "After." Everything to him was "After"—after
death, after sin, after sorrow, after frustration, after alien-
ation. Now everything had promise in it—had a future.
In sin there is no future—it is the way to decay and death.

Jesus is the Yes to all the promises of God made everywhere. There are thirty-three thousand promises in the
Scriptures, and Jesus is the Yes to every one of them. He
writes "Yes" in His own blood on every promise. If you
come in His name, you can have them cashed in experience.

E. STANLEY JONES

DAY 9

OUR LORD JESUS

2 CORINTHIANS 1:20 NLT
For all of God's promises have been fulfilled in him.
That is why we say "Amen" when we give glory
to God through Christ.

What is emphasized throughout the New Testament is that . . . all the images and motifs of
revelation and response, are fulfilled in Jesus. "We have
found him," say the Evangelists and apostolic writers
echoing Philip; this is He. . . . In Jesus the promise is confirmed, the covenant is renewed, the prophecies are fulfilled, the law is vindicated, salvation is brought near,
sacred history has reached its climax, the perfect sacrifice
has been offered and accepted, the great priest over the
household of God has taken his seat at God's right hand,
the Prophet like Moses has been raised up, the Son of
David reigns, the kingdom of God has been inaugurated,
the Son of Man has received dominion from the Ancient
of Days, the Servant of the Lord, having been smitten to
death for his people's transgression and borne the sin of
many, has accomplished the divine purpose, has seen light
after the travail of his soul and is now exalted and extolled
and made very high.

F. F. BRUCE

STANDING ON THE PROMISES

CORINTHIANS 1:20 ESV
*For all the promises of God find their Yes in him.
That is why it is through him that we utter
our Amen to God for his glory.*

Standing on the promises of Christ my King,
Through eternal ages let His praises ring;
Glory in the highest I will shout and sing,
Standing on the promises of God.

Standing on the promises that cannot fail,
When the howling storms of doubt and fears assail;
By the living Word of God I shall prevail,
Standing on the promises of God.

Standing on the promises I now can see
Perfect, present cleansing in the blood for me;
Standing in the liberty where Christ makes me free,
Standing on the promises of God.

Standing on the promises of Christ the Lord,
Bound to Him eternally by love's strong cord;
Overcoming daily with the Spirit's sword,
Standing on the promises of God.

R. KELSO CARTER

THE GLORY OF THE PROMISES

2 CORINTHIANS 1:20 KJV

*For all the promises of God in him are yea, and in him
Amen, unto the glory of God by us.*

He gives us sometimes . . . a view of himself; but it is
imperfect, as is our sight of a man through a window. The appearances of him . . . are full of refreshment
unto the souls of them that do believe. But our view of
them is imperfect, transient, and does not abide—we are
for the most part quickly left to bemoan what we have
lost. And then our best is but to cry, "the hart panteth
after the water brooks, so panteth my soul after thee,
O God. My soul thirsteth for God, for the living God:
when shall I come and appear before God?" When wilt
thou again give me to see thee, though but as through
the windows alas! . . . This displaying of the glory of
Christ . . . is by the promises of the Gospel, as they are
explained in the ministry of the Word. In them are represented unto us the desirable beauties and glories of
Christ. How precious, how amiable is he, as represented
in them! How are the souls of believers ravished with the
views of them!

JOHN OWEN

COME AND DRINK

ISAIAH 55:1–2 NLT

*Is anyone thirsty? Come and drink—even if you have
no money! Come, take your choice of wine or milk—
it's all free! Why spend your money on food that
does not give you strength? Why pay for food that
does you no good? Listen, and I will tell you
where to get food that is good for the soul!*

Expressions such as "having a relationship with God"
and "becoming a Christian" might be new to you.
I know that has been true for some of our readers, so let
me explain. Christians believe that God is a person, and
that we have personality because he does. Our hearts—
with all their yearnings—are expressions of his. We
believe that a relationship with God is not only possible,
but can be the most intimate and satisfying love we'll ever
know. Jesus of Nazareth claimed to be "God in the flesh,"
the eternal God come down to make himself known to
mankind. When he offers to slake your thirst, he means
he will come and satisfy your heart's deepest longings.
"Coming to him" means believing in him, trusting him
with your well-being now and forever.

JOHN ELDREDGE

THE JOY OF GOD

PSALM 119:162 NLT
*I rejoice in your word
like one who finds a great treasure.*

Joy belongs not only to those who have been called home, but also to the living, and no one shall take it from us. . . . I don't mean by this something fabricated, compelled, but something given, free. Joy dwells with God; it descends from him and seizes spirit, soul, and body, and where this joy has grasped a man it grows greater, carries him away, opens closed doors. There is a joy which knows nothing of sorrow, need, and anxiety of the heart; it has no duration, and it can only drug one for the moment. The joy of God has been through the poverty of the crib and the distress of the cross; therefore it is insuperable, irrefutable. It does not deny the distress where it is, but finds God in the midst of it, indeed precisely there; it does not contest the most grievous sin, but finds forgiveness in just this way; it looks death in the face, yet finds life in death itself.

DIETRICH BONHOEFFER

GOD'S OATH

HEBREWS 6:17–18 NCV

*God wanted to prove that his promise was true
to those who would get what he promised.
And he wanted them to understand clearly that
his purposes never change, so he made an oath.
These two things cannot change: God cannot lie
when he makes a promise, and he cannot lie when
he makes an oath. These things encourage us
who came to God for safety. They give us strength
to hold on to the hope we have been given.*

In Thy presence is fullness of joy; at Thy right hand there are pleasures for evermore.' It is that glorious communion with Jesus Christ of which the Apostle speaks, when he says, 'Having a desire to depart, and to be with Christ; which is far better.' It is that state in which believers shall be like Him, for they shall see Him as He is.

It is the hope of righteousness for which, through the Spirit, believers wait (Galatians 5:5). This hope is founded on the unchangeable promise of God—on His promise accompanied by His oath—on the blood of Christ with which He has sealed His promise—on Him who was not only dead, but is risen again, who is even at the right hand of God, who also maketh intercession for His people.

ROBERT HALDANE

THE PURIFYING POWER OF PROMISES

2 CORINTHIANS 7:1 ESV

*Since we have these promises, beloved, let us cleanse
ourselves from every defilement of body and spirit,
bringing holiness to completion in the fear of God.*

The essential unity of faith and obedience therefore
corresponds to the fact that the focus of faith is on
God's *promises* for our *future,* while its foundation rests
on God's *provisions* in the *past.* The provisions and promises of God bind the Creator to his creatures in such a way
that they can be called to obedience in response. Hence,
from the standpoint of the Bible, to say that we "have faith
in God" means that we are trusting in God's promises for
our future because of what God has already done for us
in the past. As Calvin said, "We make the freely given
promise of God the foundation of faith because upon
it faith properly rests. . . . Faith properly begins with the
promise, rests in it, and ends in it."

SCOTT HAFEMANN

GRATITUDE FOR GOD'S PROMISES

2 CORINTHIANS 7:1 NIV
Since we have these promises, dear friends, let us purify
ourselves from everything that contaminates body and
spirit, perfecting holiness out of reverence for God.

In His promises God takes the initiative and anticipates us by His pure grace, but having thus freely granted us His grace, He immediately requires of us gratitude in return. When He said to Abraham, 'I am thy God' (Genesis 17:7), that was an offer of His free undeserved kindness, but He added at the same time this demand, 'Walk before me and be thou perfect.' Since this second clause is not always explicit, Paul tells us that this condition is implied in all God's promises so that they should urge us on to promote God's glory. . . .

He would have us pure from defilements, not only inwardly where God alone can discern them, but also outwardly where they come under the observation of men. It is as if he had said, 'We should not only have consciences that are pure in God's sight, but we should also consecrate to Him our whole body and all our members so that no impurity can be seen in any part of us.'

JOHN CALVIN

DELIGHT IN THE PROMISES OF GOD

PSALM 119:54 NLT
*Your principles have been the music of my life
throughout the years of my pilgrimage.*

A delight in the precepts and promises of God, which are the ground and rules of prayer. First, David delights in God's testimonies and then calls upon him with his whole heart. A gracious heart must first delight in precepts and promises, before it can turn them into prayers: for prayer is nothing else but a presenting God with his own promise, desiring to work that in us and for us which he hath promised to us. None was more cheerful in prayer than David, because none was more rejoicing in the statutes of God. God's statutes were his songs (Psalm 119:54). And the divine Word was sweeter to him than the honey and the honey-comb. If our hearts leap not at divine promises, we are like to have but drowsy souls in desiring them. . . . It was the hopes of reward that made Moses so valiant in suffering, and the joy set before Christ in a promise, made him so cheerful in enduring the shame (Hebrews 12:1, 2).

STEPHEN CHARNOCK

Are the Promises for You?

JOHN 5:24 KJV

*Verily, verily, I say unto you, He that heareth my word,
and believeth on him that sent me, hath everlasting life,
and shall not come into condemnation;
but is passed from death unto life.*

Perhaps some of our readers are still ready to say, "I do not see that there needs to be so much difficulty in ascertaining whether one is in a lost or saved condition: I am resting upon John 5:24, and that is sufficient for me." . . . That John 5:24 contains a precious promise, we gladly acknowledge, but to whom is it made? Let us examine it: "Verily, verily, I say unto you, He that heareth my word, and believeth on him that sent me, hath everlasting life, and shall not come into condemnation; but is passed from death unto life."

. . . Ah, are you obedient? Have you searched the Scriptures diligently in order to discover His commandments? And that, not to satisfy an idle curiosity, but desiring to put them into practice? Do you love His commandments? Are you actually doing them? Not once or twice, but regularly, as the main tenor of your life—for note it is not "hear" but "heareth."

A. W. PINK

THE HAPPY PROMISE

2 PETER 1:3–4 ESV

His divine power has granted to us all things that
pertain to life and godliness, through the knowledge of
him who called us to his own glory and excellence,
by which he has granted to us his precious and very
great promises, so that through them you may become
partakers of the divine nature, having escaped from the
corruption that is in the world because of sinful desire.

The knowledge that leads to life and godliness is said
to be the knowledge of God's precious and very
great promises. And so we learn that the only knowledge
of God that carries saving power is promising knowledge.
The knowledge of the glory and excellence of God (in
verse 3) gives power for godliness only if it communicates
to us the happy promise that *we* are called and included.
If after a week of rain a gloomy child wakes up on Satur-
day morning and sees the glorious sunshine calling him
to play outdoors, new power flows into his spirit; but only
if he really can go outside. If he were sick and couldn't
play, the beauty of the day and the fun of his friends outside might make him miserable. The knowledge of the
glory of God must be *promising* if it is to carry power. We
must know it *and* believe that *we* are included—that the
promises are *ours*, that the call is to us.

JOHN PIPER

ARMED WITH GOD'S PROMISES

2 PETER 1:4 NASB

*For by these He has granted to us His precious
and magnificent promises, so that by them you may
become partakers of the divine nature, having
escaped the corruption that is in the world by lust.*

Very practically I think this means we must day by
day go to the Word of God and search for great
promises. Fix one or two in your mind and hold them
there before you all day. And use them to overcome
temptation to sin and to incite you to daring acts of righteousness and love. Notice in the last part of verse 4 that
corruption comes "by passion" or "lust" or "desire." This
means that the battle against corruption is fought on the
field of our desires or passions. Sin makes its attack by
holding out promises to us for our happiness: if you lie on
your income tax return, you will have more money and
be happier; if you divorce your spouse, you will be happier . . . And sin will always win the battle unless we have
the luscious carrot of *God's* promises hanging clearly in
front of our noses. Unless we enter our day armed with
one or two precious and very great promises we will be
utterly vulnerable to temptation.

JOHN PIPER

DIVINE POWER

EZRA 3:11 NLT
With praise and thanks, they sang this
song to the LORD: "He is so good!
His faithful love for Israel endures forever!"
Then all the people gave a great shout, praising
the LORD because the foundation of the
LORD'S Temple had been laid.

Their magnificent temple had been destroyed. The
city walls had been torn down. They had no resources to rebuild their splendid city. As these former
refugees looked at the mammoth task before them, they
realized their poverty and weakness, and they became
greatly dismayed. Then came God's Word! He promised
that they would, indeed, rebuild their city. But, He told
them, the rebuilding would not be accomplished by their
own power and resources but by His Spirit. . . .

There will be times when obeying God will lead you
to impossible situations. If you look at your own skills,
knowledge, and resources, you will become discouraged.
However, when you became a Christian, God placed His
Spirit within you. You now have the resources of heaven
at your disposal. The success of your endeavors will not
depend on the way you use your own resources but on
how you obey the Spirit of God.

HENRY BLACKABY AND RICHARD BLACKABY

REST IN HIM

HEBREWS 4:1 KJV
Let us therefore fear, lest, a promise being left us
of entering into his rest, any of you
should seem to come short of it.

Oh, be persuaded to hide yourself in Christ Jesus! What greater assurance of safety can you desire? He has undertaken to defend and save you, if you will come to Him. He looks upon it as His work. He engaged in it before the world was, and He has given His faithful promise which He will not break; and if you will but make your flight there, His life shall be for yours. He will answer for you, and you shall have nothing to do but rest quietly in Him. You may stand still and see what the Lord will do for you. If there is anything to suffer, the suffering is Christ's; you will have nothing to suffer. If there be anything to be done, the doing of it is Christ's; you will have nothing to do but to stand still and behold it.

JONATHAN EDWARDS

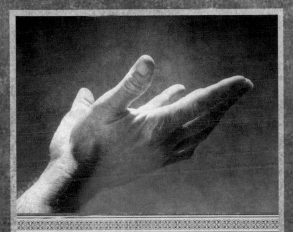

ABOUT HIS BIRTH, LIFE, DEATH, AND RESURRECTION

For to us a child is born, to us a son is given, and the government will be on his shoulders. And he will be called Wonderful Counselor, Mighty God, Everlasting Father, Prince of Peace.

Isaiah 9:6 NIV

ABOUT HIS BIRTH, LIFE, DEATH, AND RESURRECTION

Jesus came wrapped in promises. Centuries before His birth, rumors of His coming filled the mouths of Jewish prophets and crowded the pages of scripture. Many of these promises were common knowledge, at least among devout Jews. When the wise men showed up in Jerusalem looking for a child-king, Herod the Edomite had no idea what they were talking about, but the priests he consulted had a ready answer. "If there has been a king of the Jews born," they reported, "his birthplace would have to be Bethlehem."

The problem with the Messianic prophecies wasn't their precision but their interpretation. The details of Jesus' birth and life fit the pattern of promise exactly, but He didn't match the expectations of the people regarding their Messiah. As John described the situation, "He came to His own, and His own did not receive Him. But as many as received Him, to them He gave the right to become children of God, to those who believe in His name" (John 1:11–12 NKJV). Let the promises Jesus fulfilled draw you to receive Him.

HE BECAME FLESH FOR OUR SAKE

ISAIAH 7:14 NKJV

Therefore the Lord Himself will give you a sign:
Behold, the virgin shall conceive and bear a Son,
and shall call His name Immanuel.

The Word had become flesh: a real human baby. . . .
He who made the angel who became the devil was
now in a state in which He could be tempted—could
not, indeed, avoid being tempted—by the devil; and the
perfection of His human life was only achieved by conflict with the devil. The Epistle to the Hebrews, looking
up to Him in His ascended glory, draws great comfort
from this fact. 'In all things it behoved him to be made
like unto his brethren . . . For in that he himself hath suffered being tempted, *he is able to help them that are tempted.*'
"We have not an high priest which cannot be touched
with the feeling of our infirmities, but was in all points
tempted like as we are, yet without sin. Let us *therefore*
come boldly unto the throne of grace, that we may obtain
mercy, and find grace to help in time of need" (Hebrews
2:17–18, 4:15–16).

J. I. PACKER

BETHLEHEM IN OUR HEARTS

ISAIAH 7:14 NLT
All right then, the Lord himself will choose the sign.
Look! The virgin will conceive a child!
She will give birth to a son and will call him
Immanuel—"God is with us."

So the holy one to be born will be called the Son of God" (Luke 1:35). Jesus Christ was born *into* this world, not from it. . . . His life is the Highest and the Holiest entering in at the Lowliest door. Our Lord's birth was an advent.

His birth in me. "For whom I am again in the pains of childbirth until Christ is formed in you" (Galations 4:19). Just as our Lord came into human history from outside, so He must come into me from outside. Have I allowed my personal human life to become a "Bethlehem" for the Son of God? I cannot enter into the realm of the Kingdom of God unless I am born from above by a birth totally unlike natural birth. "You must be born again." This is not a command, it is a foundation fact. The characteristic of the new birth is that I yield myself so completely to God that Christ is formed in me.

OSWALD CHAMBERS

TRULY GOD AND TRULY HUMAN

LUKE 2:6–7 ESV

*And while they were there, the time came for her
to give birth. And she gave birth to her firstborn son
and wrapped him in swaddling cloths and laid him
in a manger, because there was no place
for them in the inn.*

The virgin birth of Christ is an unmistakable reminder
that salvation can never come through human effort,
but must be the work of God himself.

The virgin birth made possible the uniting of full deity
and full humanity in one person. . . . If we think for a
moment of other possible ways in which Christ might
have come to the earth, none of them would so clearly
unite humanity and deity in one person. . . .

The virgin birth also makes possible Christ's true
humanity without inherited sin. . . . All human beings
have inherited legal guilt and a corrupt moral nature from
their first father, Adam (this is sometimes called "inherited sin" or "original sin"). But the fact that Jesus did not
have a human father means that the line of descent from
Adam is partially interrupted. . . . And this helps us to
understand why the legal guilt and moral corruption that
belongs to all other human beings did not belong to
Christ.

WAYNE GRUDEM

THE CHILD OF PROMISE

ISAIAH 9:6 NRSV

*For a child has been born for us, a son given to us;
authority rests upon his shoulders; and he is named
Wonderful Counselor, Mighty God,
Everlasting Father, Prince of Peace.*

Consider, again, the incarnation of Christ, and you will rightly say that his name deserveth to be called "Wonderful." Oh! what is that I see? Oh! world of wonders, what is that I see? The Eternal of ages, whose hair is white like wool, as white as snow, becomes an infant. Can it be? Ye angels, are ye not astonished? He becomes an infant, hangs at a virgin's breast, draws his nourishment from the breast of woman. Oh wonder of wonders! Manger of Bethlehem, thou hast miracles poured into thee. This is a sight that surpasses all others. Talk ye of the sun, moon, and stars; consider ye the heavens, the work of God's fingers, the moon and the stars that he hath ordained; but all the wonders of the universe shrink into nothing, when we come to the mystery of the incarnation of the Lord Jesus Christ.

C. H. SPURGEON

THE CRADLE AND THE CROSS

MICAH 5:2 ESV

But you, O Bethlehem Ephrathah, who are too little
to be among the clans of Judah, from you shall come
forth for me one who is to be ruler in Israel,
whose origin is from of old, from ancient days.

If Christmas means anything to you, then it must mean
everything. It is a beginning and an end. It is a time of
darkness and inexpressible light. It is a time of blessed
relief at finally seeing all God's promises come true in one
person. It is a time of tension as well, as we look ahead in
the life of this dear little one with a kind of historical
omnipresence because we know how it all will end, on
earth anyway. As our family gathers around our faint,
flickering candle to read the Christmas story, the loneliness of the stable reminds us of the loneliness of another
place on a hill outside Jerusalem. . . .

Celebrate? you say. Yes, most heartily, amidst the dung
of the stable, which is, of course, the refuse of the world.
Celebrate at the foot of that ghastly cross because it is the
hope of the world. Gather around a cattle trough and
celebrate a baby born in poverty and rejected because He
is the Savior of the world!

MICHAEL CARD

LED BY GOD

LUKE 2:15 NASB

*When the angels had gone away from them into heaven,
that the shepherds began saying to one another,
"Let us go straight to Bethlehem then, and see
this thing that has happened which
the Lord has made known to us."*

Luke relates how it came to pass that Christ was born in the city of Bethlehem even though His mother Mary lived elsewhere nearly to the time of her delivery. . . . As their only purpose was to conform to Augustus' edict, we should properly understand that it was by the hand of God they were led—like blind people—to the place where Christ was to be born. . . . It should occur to us to think of what was predicted many centuries before by the Prophet, where comparison will clearly show, that this was not without the wonderful providence of God, that a census was then ordered by Caesar Augustus, and that Joseph and Mary set foot from home, in order that they might reach Bethlehem at exactly the right moment. Thus we see that there are times when the saintly servants of God, though their purpose be uncertain, and they wander unaware of where their steps lead, yet keep to the right road, as God directs their path.

JOHN CALVIN

THE WORD WAS MADE FLESH

LUKE 3:4-6 ESV

As it is written in the book of the words of Isaiah the prophet,
"The voice of one crying in the wilderness:
'Prepare the way of the Lord, make his paths straight.
Every valley shall be filled, . . . and all flesh
shall see the salvation of God.'"

It is not the case that all our ways lead to God. He has marked out definite paths for us so that we may know and acknowledge that salvation is his grace, his free, gratuitous grace and not a right of our own, something he owes us. . . . He has marked out definite ways of salvation for us because he himself—grace beyond all measure! — willed to walk them, because he himself willed to become a human being, caught like us in space and time and history from which in truth no human mind can extricate itself in this world. . . .

In fact Christianity is so human and so historical that it is too human for many people, who think that the true religion must be inhuman, i.e., not of the senses, nonhistorical. But the Word was made flesh. The word of the Lord went forth to John in the fifteenth year of the Emperor Tiberius. And so it has remained.

KARL RAHNER

THE DAY HAS COME

LUKE 4:16, 18 NIV
And he stood up to read. . . .

*"The Spirit of the Lord is on me, because he has
anointed me to preach good news to the poor.
He has sent me to proclaim freedom
for the prisoners . . ."*

Did he choose the passage himself, or was it the set reading for the day? It is hard to say. . . . At any rate, whether set or not, the passage was a very significant one. It describes the work of God's "anointed one." It was one of many Old Testament passages in which the Jews of that time found a description of the work of the Messiah ("anointed one"), the deliverer whom God was going to send to his people, and whom they were eagerly expecting.

There was a pregnant pause. "All the people in the synagogue had their eyes fixed on him," says Luke. No doubt some of them guessed what was coming.

"Then he began to speak to them: 'This passage of scripture has come true today, as you heard it being read.'" There it is, simple, clear, unmistakable—and breath-taking. The carpenter is claiming to be the Messiah. . . . The great day has come. And it has come, of all places, in Nazareth.

R. T. FRANCE

OUR HANDS DROVE THE NAILS

ISAIAH 53:5 NIV

But he was pierced for our transgressions, he was crushed for our iniquities; the punishment that brought us peace was upon him, and by his wounds we are healed.

There is a strange conspiracy of silence in the world today—even in religious circles—about man's responsibility for sin, the reality of judgment and about an outraged God and the necessity for a crucified Savior. . . .

Let us not eloquently blame Judas nor Pilate. . . .

Let us not curse the Jews for delivering Jesus to be crucified. Let us not single out the Romans in blaming them for putting Jesus on the cross.

Oh, they were guilty, certainly! But they were our accomplices in crime. They and we put Him on the cross, not they alone. That rising malice and anger that burns so hotly in your being today put Him there. That basic dishonesty that comes to light in your being when you knowingly cheat and chisel on your income tax return—that put Him on the cross. The evil, the hatred, the suspicion, the jealousy, the lying tongue, the carnality, the fleshly love of pleasure—all of these in natural man joined in putting Him on the cross.

A. W. TOZER

THE JUST FOR THE UNJUST

1 PETER 2:24 NRSV

He himself bore our sins in his body on the cross,
so that, free from sins, we might live for righteousness;
by his wounds you have been healed.

Jesus has borne the death penalty on our behalf. Behold the wonder! There He hangs upon the cross! This is the greatest sight you will ever see. Son of God and Son of man, there He hangs, bearing pains unutterable, the Just for the unjust, to bring us to God. Oh the glory of that sight! The Innocent punished! The Holy One condemned! The ever-blessed One made a curse! The infinitely glorious One put to a shameful death! The more I look at the sufferings of the Son of God, the more sure I am that they must meet my case. Why did He suffer if not to turn aside the penalty from us? If, then, He turned it aside by His death, it is turned aside; and those who believe in Him need not fear it. It must be so that since expiation is made, God is able to forgive without shaking the basis of His throne or in the least degree blotting the statute book. Conscience gets a full answer to her tremendous question.

C. H. SPURGEON

DAY 33

THE SUFFERING SERVANT

ISAIAH 53:6 NASB

*All of us like sheep have gone astray, each of us
has turned to his own way; but the LORD has caused
the iniquity of us all to fall on Him.*

Franz Delitzsch made an extraordinary but true com-
ment about the 53rd chapter of Isaiah when he said
that this chapter is "the most central, the deepest, and the
loftiest thing that the Old Testament prophecy, outstrip-
ping itself, has ever achieved." When a Christian reads
Isaiah 53 he is struck by how amazingly the chapter
describes what our Savior Jesus Christ went through in
His sufferings, death, resurrection and ascension. In contrast to this, when an unbelieving Jewish person today
reads this chapter, if he reads it at all, he sees a description
of the nation of Israel, especially since more than likely his
local rabbi has made it clear to him that this is the
"proper" Jewish interpretation of this chapter.

Since the Servant in this 53rd chapter suffers voluntarily for the sins of other people and then dies, resulting in
our well-being, who else could the Servant refer to
except Messiah Jesus?

DAVID R. BREWER

THE SECOND ADAM

ISAIAH 53:6 NLT

*All of us have strayed away like sheep. We have
left God's paths to follow our own. Yet the LORD
laid on him the guilt and sins of us all.*

Understanding the faultlessness of Jesus is central to
our understanding of the cross. For an atonement
to be acceptable to God, it was necessary that the sacrificial lamb had to be without blemish. The utter sinlessness
of Jesus qualified Him to be our Savior. The death of a
man was not sufficient to pay the penalty prescribed by
the law of God. It had to be a *sinless* man. Had Jesus' character been marred by a single transgression, He would not
have qualified to save us by His death.

It is the life of Christ that is as crucial for our redemption as His death. God did not simply send His incarnate
Son immediately from heaven, full grown, and execute
Him on the spot at the moment of His arrival. Before
Christ could die for us He had to first live for us. As the
new Adam, He had to pass the test of the Law. His life of
perfect obedience was a necessary prerequisite for His
perfect sacrifice.

R. C. SPROUL

CHRIST'S SOVEREIGN POWER

LUKE 23:44–45 ESV
*It was now about the sixth hour, and there
was darkness over the whole land until the
ninth hour, while the sun's light failed.
And the curtain of the temple was torn in two.*

O the marvellous power of the cross, the glory in the passion! No tongue can fully describe it. Here . . . sentence is passed upon the world, and here the sovereignty of the Crucified is revealed. You drew all things to yourself, Lord, when you stretched out your hands all the day long to a people that denied and opposed you, until at last the whole world was brought to proclaim your majesty. You drew all things to yourself, Lord, when all the elements combined to pronounce judgment in execration of that crime; when the lights of heaven were darkened and the day was turned into night; when the land was shaken by unwonted earthquakes, and all creation refused to serve those wicked people. Yes, Lord, you drew all things to yourself; the veil of the temple was torn in two and the Holy of Holies taken away from those unworthy high priests. . . . Through your cross the faithful are given strength instead of weakness, glory instead of shame, life instead of death.

LEO THE GREAT

SILENCE IN SUFFERING

ISAIAH 53:7 NASB
*He was oppressed and He was afflicted, yet He did not
open His mouth; like a lamb that is led to slaughter,
and like a sheep that is silent before its shearers,
so He did not open His mouth.*

The evidence that the Servant patiently, willingly
accepted all the suffering is seen in His behavior during the suffering. This patient suffering is brought out
vividly by total lack of self-defense. There was no self-defense, protest, or complaint. How strange this behavior is
in comparison to our generation that plays the blame game
in just about everything. . . .

Jesus Christ, the Suffering Servant, was not resentful or
rebellious toward His sufferings. He chose to suffer and to
do so in silent submission to the will of God. He patiently
suffered voluntarily.

The expression, "He opened not His mouth," is a
comparison of the Servant to a lamb. Shepherds shear
sheep while they stand silently. They lead them to the
slaughter and they open not their mouths. There is no
bleating; they stand there in dumb silence. The Servant
endured all His suffering patiently without a word of
protest or complaint.

WIL POUNDS

He Made No Defense

Matthew 27:12 NASB
And while He was being accused by the chief priests and elders, He did not answer.

The reason for the Evangelist's saying that Christ kept quiet, when we have just heard His reply come from their lips, is that He voluntarily kept from using the defence He had prepared. His earlier answer about the Kingdom was not to win release, but only to assert that He was the Redeemer, long-promised, before whose Face every knee should bow. Pilate wondered at His patience, that Christ by silence should let His innocence suffer when He might have been ready to refute the heartless and empty slanders. Christ's integrity was such that the judge saw it clearly without an advocate. . . . In case we should wonder at Christ's silence, thinking what He did strange, we should hold on to the purpose of God who was willing for His Son (whom He had appointed to be victim, for the expiation of our sins), though pure in Himself, to be found guilty on our behalf. Christ kept silence, to be our spokesman now, and by His pleading to free us of our guilt.

John Calvin

OPPRESSION AND JUDGMENT

ISAIAH 53:8 NIV
*By oppression and judgment he was taken away.
And who can speak of his descendants? For he was cut
off from the land of the living; for the transgression
of my people he was stricken.*

It is a striking thing that in the gospel accounts of the trials of Jesus he never spoke up on his own behalf or tried to escape the penalty. This amazed both Pilate and Caiaphas. When our Lord stood before the High Priest, he was silent until the High Priest put him on oath to tell them who he was. When he stood before Pilate, he was silent until to remain silent was to deny his very Kingship. Then he spoke briefly, acknowledging who he was. . . .

It is very apparent to anyone reading the gospel accounts that the trials that Jesus went through were a farce. The Jewish trial before the High Priest was illegal. It was held at night, which was contrary to the law. Pilate several times admitted that he could find no wrong in him, and yet he pronounced upon him the sentence of death. How true are these words, "by oppression and judgment he was taken away."

RAY C. STEDMAN

CONFIDENCE IN DEATH

ISAIAH 53:12 NLT

*I will give him the honors of one who is mighty and
great, because he exposed himself to death. He was
counted among those who were sinners. He bore
the sins of many and interceded for sinners.*

A ll three of the prayers from the cross are tied to
Scripture. When Jesus prayed, "Father, forgive
them; for they know not what they do" (Luke 23:34), He
was fulfilling Isaiah 53:12: "He . . . made intercession for
the transgressors." When He cried out, "My God, my
God, why hast thou forsaken me" (Matthew 27:46), He
was quoting Psalm 22:1. When He said, "Father, into thy
hands I commend my spirit" (Luke 23:46), He fulfilled
Psalm 31:5. Our Lord Jesus lived by God's Word, and if
you live by God's Word, you can *die* by God's Word. What
assurance do you have that you will experience confidence in death? The only assurance we have is the Word
of God. He died confidently with the Father's presence
and with the Father's promise.

WARREN W. WIERSBE

INTERCESSION FOR THE TRANSGRESSORS

LUKE 23:34 NIV
*Jesus said, "Father, forgive them, for they
do not know what they are doing."*

How much God made known beforehand of what should transpire on that Day of days! What a complete picture did the Holy Spirit furnish of our Lord's Passion with all the attendant circumstances! Among other things it had been foretold that the Saviour should "make intercession for the transgressors" (Isaiah 53:12). This did not have reference to the present ministry of Christ at God's right hand. It is true that "He is able also to save them to the uttermost that come unto God by Him, seeing He ever liveth to make intercession for them" (Hebrews 7:25), but . . . Isaiah 53:12 had reference to His gracious act at the time of His crucifixion. Observe what His intercession for the transgressors is there linked with—"And He was numbered with the transgressors; and He bare the sin of many, and made intercession for the transgressors."

. . . He thought for His murderers. He pleaded for His crucifiers . . .

"Then said Jesus, 'Father, forgive them, for they know not what they do.'"

A. W. PINK

THE GENIUS OF CHRIST'S SACRIFICE

1 CORINTHIANS 1:30 NKJV
*But of Him you are in Christ Jesus, who became
for us wisdom from God—and righteousness
and sanctification and redemption.*

Where is the wisdom of God here? It is found in this: God's incarnate Son has identified himself with us in such a way that he is able to represent us, indeed substitute himself in our place before God's judgement and under his wrath. . . . In the outward darkness of Golgotha, the Son of God experienced the *inner* darkness of his own Father's rejection. Utterly alone he entered the dark night of death as sin's penalty. He bore that for us.

Yet here the divine master-stroke appears. Because he was the *incarnate* Son of God, he was able to die as one of us in our place. But because he was the perfect and holy *Son of God,* death did not have the power to restrain him in its grip. The wisdom of God was seen in this: what appeared at first to be a human tragedy—Jesus' death— was, in fact, the key to the divine strategy and the prelude to his resurrection.

SINCLAIR B. FERGUSON

THE BLOOD OF THE LAMB

MARK 10:45 ESV

For even the Son of Man came not to be served but to serve, and to give his life as a ransom for many.

Oh! who shall measure the heights of the Saviour's all-sufficiency? . . . The flood of Christ's redemption prevails over the tops of the mountains of our sins. In Heaven's courts there are today men that once were murderers, and thieves, and drunkards, and whoremongers, and blasphemers, and persecutors; but they have been washed—they have been sanctified. Ask them whence the brightness of their robes hath come, and where their purity hath been achieved, and they, with united breath, tell you that they have washed their robes, and made them white in the blood of the Lamb. O ye troubled consciences! O ye weary and heavy-laden ones! O ye that are groaning on account of sin! the great redemption now proclaimed to you is all-sufficient for your wants; and though your numerous sins exceed the stars that deck the sky, here is an atonement made for them all—a river which can overflow the whole of them, and carry them away from you for ever.

C. H. SPURGEON

MARRED BEYOND RECOGNITION

ISAIAH 52:14 NIV

Just as there were many who were appalled at him—
his appearance was so disfigured beyond that of any man
and his form marred beyond human likeness . . .

By the time these serial beatings were completed, do you see how Isaiah 52:14 perfectly describes our Savior? The prophet declared that many "were appalled at him— / his appearance was so disfigured beyond that of any man / and his form marred beyond human likeness." Those were no poetic descriptions. The words are a stark depiction of the reality of the most precious face ever to grace this planet.

Stripped. Mocked. Spat upon. Struck . . . again and again. Flogged. Beyond recognition. The fullness of the Godhead bodily. The bright and morning Star. The Alpha and Omega. The anointed of the Lord. The beloved Son of God. The radiance of His Father's glory. The Light of the world. The Hope of glory. The Lily of the valley. The Prince of peace. The Seed of David. The Son of righteousness. . . .

The most terrifying truth a mocking humanity will ever confront is that no matter how Jesus is belittled, He cannot be made little. He is the King of the mountain.

BETH MOORE

WE WERE THERE

MATTHEW 26:67 NKJV

Then they spat in His face and beat Him; and others struck Him with the palms of their hands.

Were you there when they crucified my Lord? Yes, we were there when we crucified our Lord. . . . In ways I do not fully understand, I know that I, too, did the deed, wielded the whip, drove the nails, thrust the spear.

About chief of sinners I don't know, but what I know about sinners I know chiefly about me. We did not mean to do the deed, of course. The things we have done wrong seemed, or mostly seemed, small at the time. The word of encouragement withheld, the touch of kindness not given, the visit not made, the trust betrayed, the cutting remark so clever and so cruel, the illicit sexual desire so generously entertained, the angry answer, the surge of resentment at being slighted, the lie we thought would do no harm. . . . But now it has come to this. It has come to the cross. All the trespasses of all the people of all time have gravitated here, to the killing grounds of Calvary.

RICHARD JOHN NEUHAUS

CRUCIFIXION

LUKE 23:33 NASB
*When they came to the place called The Skull,
there they crucified Him and the criminals,
one on the right and the other on the left.*

We do not need to hold that Jesus suffered more physical pain than any human being has ever suffered, for the Bible nowhere makes such a claim. But we still must not forget that death by crucifixion was one of the most horrible forms of execution ever devised by man.

. . . A criminal who was crucified was essentially forced to inflict upon himself a very slow death by suffocation. When the criminal's arms were outstretched and fastened by nails to the cross, he had to support most of the weight of his body with his arms. The chest cavity would be pulled upward and outward, making it difficult to exhale in order to be able to draw a fresh breath. But when the victim's longing for oxygen became unbearable, he would have to push himself up with his feet, . . . but it was extremely painful because it required putting the body's weight on the nails holding the feet, and bending the elbows and pulling upward on the nails driven through the wrists.

WAYNE GRUDEM

FATHER, FORGIVE THEM

LUKE 23:33–34 NRSV

When they came to the place that is called The Skull, they crucified Jesus there with the criminals, one on his right and one on his left. Then Jesus said, "Father, forgive them; for they do not know what they are doing."

Captain Mitsuo Fuchida was the commander of the squadron that bombed Pearl Harbor on December 7, 1941. After the war he became a hero in Japan, yet he felt his life was empty. Then he heard the amazing story of one of the American fliers, Jacob DeShazer, one of Doolittle's bombers, who had been captured and put in prison in Japan. At first he was a very intractable prisoner, but someone gave him a New Testament and, reading it, his whole life was changed.

Fuchida heard about that change in the life of DeShazer, and Fuchida himself began to read the New Testament. . . . He was so moved by the prayer that broke from the lips of Jesus as he hung upon the cross with his torturers and tormentors gathered about him, "Father, forgive them for they know not what they do" (Luke 23:34), that his own heart broke. . . . In that moment he opened his heart to Christ, and ultimately became a Christian evangelist.

RAY C. STEDMAN

THE OTHER CRIMINAL

LUKE 23:39–40, 42 NIV
One of the criminals who hung there hurled insults at him: "Aren't you the Christ? Save yourself and us!" But the other criminal rebuked him. . . . Then he said, "Jesus, remember me when you come into your kingdom."

He confessed his guilt, concealing nothing and making a clean breast of it all. With real sorrow of heart he looked back over the whole fearful panorama of the past and sincerely admitted that the punishment was just and deserved, the due reward of his deeds. . . .

The more he looked at Jesus and pondered all that he saw and heard there, the words and acts of Jesus on the Via Dolorosa, His prayer for His enemies, His holy majesty, the taunts and jibes of the angry mob with their references to His messiahship, the more he was convinced of the truth of Jesus' divinity and sinlessness. . . . In implicit trust he cast himself solely on Jesus' mercy, in whom he recognized not only the Mediator of salvation, but even the One who held in His pierced hands the keys of death and hell, and to whom he now appealed in faith: "Jesus, remember me, when Thou comest into Thy kingdom."

W. L. SPIELMAN

HE SUFFERED AS ONE OF US

PSALM 69:20–21 ESV

Reproaches have broken my heart, so that I am in despair. I looked for pity, but there was none, and for comforters, but I found none. They gave me poison for food, and for my thirst they gave me sour wine to drink.

In the cry, "I thirst!" we note also the setting forth of Jesus as The Perfect Son of Man. It is "the cry of the human." In our contemplation of Jesus we must never lose sight of his perfect humanity. . . .

Why did he not call to the rescue his illimitable power in this moment of pain? Why was it necessary that he should thirst? . . . Rivers were rolling to the sea; clouds full of water were floating overhead; legions of unseen angels were round about his cross, ready to minister to him; yet in this supreme moment of anguish there was not a drop for his thirsty lips. He must keep his Godhood in reserve, that he may enter into the full sorrows of humanity. Aye, he can be touched with a feeling of our infirmities. He was "in all points" such as we are. He was very man of very man.

DAVID JAMES BURNELL

THE GREAT SACRIFICE

MATTHEW 27:34 NLT
*The soldiers gave him wine mixed with bitter gall,
but when he had tasted it, he refused to drink it.*

And consider now not only the life that Jesus sacrificed for us, but consider also what the sacrifice involved. To get to the point where he could die, Jesus had to plan for it. He left the glory of heaven and took on human nature so that he could hunger and get weary and in the end suffer and die. The incarnation was the preparation of nerve endings for the nails of the cross. Jesus needed a broad human back for a place to be scourged. He needed a brow and skull as a place for the thorns. He needed cheeks for Judas' kiss and soldiers' spit. He needed hands and feet for spikes. He needed a side as a place for the sword to pierce. And he needed a brain and a spinal cord, with no vinegar and no gall, so that he could feel the entire excruciating death—for you.

JOHN PIPER

JESUS KNOWS OUR PAIN

MATTHEW 27:34 ESV
*They offered him wine to drink, mixed with gall,
but when he tasted it, he would not drink it.*

The high priest in the Old Testament, when he was ministering in the tabernacle or the temple, was warned not to drink strong drink. When our Lord Jesus Christ offered Himself as the sacrifice for sin, He did not want in any way to be identified with strong drink—He was in full control of Himself. He was the suffering Son of Man.

Do you know what this means for us today? It means that Jesus Christ is able to empathize completely with us, to identify with our pain and our need and our hurt. . . .

Wherever I go, I find people who are hurting. There is physical pain, there is emotional pain, there are spiritual burdens and battles. My Lord, the suffering Son of Man, who cried, "I thirst," has identified Himself with our every need. That encourages me to pray. . . . That encourages me not to quit, because I can come at any time to the throne of grace and find grace to help in the time of need.

WARREN W. WIERSBE

BATTLE SCARS

JOHN 19:34 NIV
Instead, one of the soldiers pierced Jesus' side with a
spear, bringing a sudden flow of blood and water.

Other religions have preached good things, but they have no Savior who can take these things and implant them in the human heart and make them grow. All other religions are built around principles, but the Christian religion is built around a person Jesus Christ, the Son of God, our Savior. Every other religion on earth is a religion you must keep, but the Christian religion saves you, keeps you, and presents you faultless before his throne. Oh, Christians! Have you any scars to show that you have fought in this conflict with the devil? When a war is over, heroes have scars to show; one rolls back his sleeve and shows a gunshot wound; another pulls down his collar and shows a wound on the neck . . . Christ has scars to show—scars on his brow, on his hands, on his feet, and when he pulls aside his robes of royalty, there will be seen the scar on his side.

BILLY SUNDAY

RISEN INDEED

PSALM 16:9–10 ESV

Therefore my heart is glad, and my whole being rejoices;
my flesh also dwells secure. For you will not abandon
my soul to Sheol, or let your holy one see corruption.

David was prophesying as a prophet the resurrection of Jesus Christ. It was Jesus Christ whose flesh would abide in hope, whose soul would not be abandoned in Hades, and who as the Holy One would never undergo decay. It was Jesus Christ who would be given back the path of life and would come back full of gladness face-to-face into the presence of God. David didn't fulfill that. His tomb is still sealed over there near Siloam. But David was a prophet and David was predicting the resurrection of Messiah. . . .

The Old Testament then in Psalm 16 predicts the resurrection of the Messiah. If the Messiah doesn't rise—if Jesus Christ doesn't rise from the grave—the Bible is not telling us the truth. But the resurrection of Christ proves that the Bible speaks truth.

JOHN MACARTHUR

RISEN TO ETERNAL LIFE

LUKE 24:46 KJV
And said unto them, Thus it is written,
and thus it behoved Christ to suffer,
and to rise from the dead the third day.

One thing is certain: if He was God and nothing else, His immortality means nothing to us; if He was man and no more, His death is no more important than yours or mine. But if He really was both God and man, then when the man Jesus died, God died too, and when the God Jesus rose from the dead, man rose too, because they were one and the same person.

The Church binds us to no theory about the exact composition of Christ's Resurrection Body. . . . It may have been made from the same elements as the body that disappeared so strangely from the guarded tomb, but it was not that old, limited, mortal body, though it was recognizably like it. In any case, those who saw the risen Christ remained persuaded that life was worth living and death a triviality—an attitude curiously unlike that of the modern defeatist, who is firmly persuaded that life is a disaster and death (rather inconsistently) a major catastrophe.

DOROTHY L. SAYERS

THE RISEN CHRIST

PSALM 110:1 NRSV
The LORD says to my lord, "Sit at my right hand until I make your enemies your footstool."

The Gospels contain abundant testimony to the resurrection of Christ (see Matthew 28:1–20; Mark 16:1–8; Luke 24:1–53; John 20:1–21:25). In addition to these detailed narratives in the four gospels, the book of Acts is a story of the apostles' proclamation of the resurrection of Christ and of continued prayer to Christ and trust in him as the one who is alive and reigning in heaven. The Epistles depend entirely on the assumption that Jesus is a living, reigning Savior who is now the exalted head of the church, who is to be trusted, worshiped, and adored, and who will some day return in power and great glory to reign as King over the earth. The book of Revelation repeatedly shows the risen Christ reigning in heaven and predicts his return to conquer his enemies and reign in glory. Thus the entire New Testament bears witness to the resurrection of Christ.

WAYNE GRUDEM

CHRIST'S HOMECOMING

PSALM 110:1 NLT
*The LORD said to my Lord, "Sit in honor
at my right hand until I humble your enemies,
making them a footstool under your feet."*

It was necessary that He should pass from the earthly
scene and return to His native heaven. The disciples
must know, the world must know, the ages to come must
know that this little planet is not all of God's great universe. Away beyond the blue dome of heaven, . . . beyond
the last gasp of dying agony, the moldering grave and the
mourner's tear—there is another realm, there is a greater
and a better world, . . . the home of God and the great
metropolis of His mighty universe. And when He had
passed through every stage of earthly experience from the
cradle to the grave, He passed on and took His place at
the right hand of God amid glorious angels and ransomed
men. It was necessary that the children of God should
realize through the ascension of their living Head that this
old earth is not their home; but, like their Master's, their
citizenship, too, is in heaven.

A. B. SIMPSON

Jesus Brings the Kingdom

Mark 10:45 esv

"For even the Son of Man came not to be served but to serve, and to give his life as a ransom for many."

The imagery of deliverance, of rescuing, of being set free—this imagery forms an important, indeed a crucial part of how the New Testament describes the saving and atoning work of Jesus. . . . He inaugurates the Kingdom of God, His Father, by taking on the forces of the evil one. His mighty works of healing the sick, exorcizing the demon-possessed, opening the eyes of the blind and the ears of the deaf—these are signs to those who have eyes to see that the Kingdom of God has broken into human affairs. God has intervened decisively on the side of man. So Jesus is the strong man who comes to snatch back the ill-gotten booty of Beelzebub (Matthew 12:29–30). Being a sinner is like being a slave to sin, to death, to the Devil (Romans 6:5–14; John 8:30–36). And the truth and the Son will set us free, and we will be really free.

Desmond Tutu

ABOUT
SALVATION

"And there is salvation in no one else;
for there is no other name under heaven
that has been given among men
by which we must be saved."

ACTS 4:12 NASB

ABOUT SALVATION

Promises often involve what we cannot do for ourselves. Our inability forces us to ask, "Can someone help me? Will someone help me? Why would someone help me?" God's promises remind us of His faithfulness during those moments when appearances give us a different message.

We often hesitate to acknowledge our sinfulness because we harbor deep doubts about the possibility of outside help. This is why God communicates His love and grace to us alongside His free offer of salvation. Still, we struggle to voice our fundamental question—"What must I do to be saved?" We dread the arduous task that we think lies ahead. We struggle to grasp God's simple response, "You can do nothing. I promise to save you. I've already done the work necessary. Trust me." On the pages that follow, the meditations on God's promises regarding salvation will offer some healthy challenges to that part of you that hesitates to trust God.

TRUST IN GOD

JOHN 3:16 NIV

"For God so loved the world that he gave his
one and only Son, that whoever believes in him
shall not perish but have eternal life."

I want to call your attention . . . to the word "trust," and to prove from the Scripture that this is all the soul has got to do to be saved—simply to trust Him. . . . A great many say, "What do you mean when you say, 'Believe in the Lord Jesus Christ?'" We mean to trust him for salvation, for strength, for every thing. He says he will keep him in perfect peace whose mind is stayed on him. The great trouble with inquirers is that their minds are stayed on themselves. They sit looking at themselves and don't get any strength, any light, any victory, and they never will till they get outside of themselves. . . . Only, instead of putting our trust in men or in princes, we are to put it in God, and he will give us perfect peace. Psalm 62:8, tells us, "Trust in him at all times; ye people, pour out your heart before him: God is a refuge for us."

DWIGHT L. MOODY

WHOEVER BELIEVES

JOHN 3:16 NLT
*"For God so loved the world that he gave his only Son,
so that everyone who believes in him
will not perish but have eternal life."*

T*hat whosoever believeth on him should not perish.* The outstanding thing about faith is that it delivers us from eternal destruction. For He especially wanted to say that although we seem to have been born for death, sure deliverance is offered to us by the faith of Christ so that we must not fear the death which otherwise threatens us. . . .

Moreover, let us remember that although life is promised generally to all who believe in Christ, faith is not common to all. Christ is open to all and displayed to all, but God opens the eyes only of the elect that they may seek Him by faith. The wonderful effect of faith is shown here too. By it we receive Christ as He is given to us by the Father—the one who has freed us from the condemnation of eternal death and made us heirs of eternal life by expiating our sins through the sacrifice of His death, so that nothing shall prevent God's acknowledging us as His children.

T. H. L. PARKER

THE TWO ROADS

MATTHEW 7:13–14 NIV

*"Enter through the narrow gate. For wide is the gate
and broad is the road that leads to destruction, and
many enter through it. But small is the gate and narrow
the road that leads to life, and only a few find it."*

One way is easy. . . . It has no curbs, no boundaries of
either thought or conduct. Travellers on this road
follow their own inclinations, that is, the desires of the
human heart in its fallenness. Superficiality, self-love,
hypocrisy, mechanical religion, false ambition, censorious-
ness—these things do not have to be learnt or cultivated.
Effort is needed to resist them. No effort is required to
practise them. That is why the broad road is easy.

The *hard* way, on the other hand, is narrow. Its boundaries are clearly marked. Its narrowness is due to something called "divine revelation," which restricts pilgrims
to the confines of what God has revealed in Scripture to
be true and good. . . .

The hard way, entered by the narrow gate, leads to *life*,
even to that "eternal life" which Jesus explained in terms
of fellowship with God, beginning here but perfected
hereafter, in which we see and share his glory, and find
perfect fulfilment as human beings in the selfless service
of him and of our fellows.

JOHN STOTT

DAY 60

LOOK FORWARD TO HEAVEN

COLOSSIANS 3:1–2 NKJV
*If then you were raised with Christ,
seek those things which are above, where Christ is,
sitting at the right hand of God. Set your mind
on things above, not on things on the earth.*

The one peaceful and trustworthy tranquillity, the one solid, firm, and constant security is this: to withdraw from the currents of a distracting world and to lift your eyes from earth to heaven, anchored in the harbor of salvation. Those who have received the gift of God and whose minds are very near to God can boast that they are completely unconcerned with the human things others elevate. . . . How heavenly is this protection and its constant blessings—to be freed from the snares of this entangling world, cleansed from earthly muck, and made suitable for the light of eternal life! By being allowed to know and condemn what we were, we are forced to love even more what we will be. . . . When the soul, in its gaze into heaven, has recognized its Author, it rises higher than the sun and far exceeds all earthly power. It begins to be that which it believes itself to be.

CYPRIAN

RANSOM

*"For even the Son of Man did not come to be served,
but to serve, and to give His life a ransom for many."*

I n this *the Son of man* is an example, not in that his disciples can also give their lives as a ransom, but in the
attitude of service (putting others first) which inspired his
unique self-sacrifice. The form of our service will be different from his, but its motivation must be the same, *not
to be served but to serve.* It was his special mission to fulfil the
role of God's *servant* in Isaiah 52:13 53:12, whose life
would be given for the sins of his people. The phrase *to
give his life as a ransom for many* is one of the clearest statements in the New Testament of the saving effect of Jesus'
death. *Lytron* ("ransom") and the preposition *anti* ("for,"
literally "instead of") point clearly to the idea of his "taking our place," as the payment of an equivalent sum of
money procures the release of the captive (or, in the Old
Testament, the "redemption" of what was dedicated to
God: see Leviticus 27 for relevant legislation).

R. T. FRANCE

THE EFFECTS OF TRUE FAITH

ROMANS 10:9 ESV

If you confess with your mouth that
Jesus is Lord and believe in your heart that
God raised him from the dead, you will be saved.

With the mouth confession is made unto salvation."
It may appear strange that Paul now ascribes part
of our salvation to faith, after having declared so frequently on previous occasions that we are saved by faith
alone. We should not, however, conclude from this that
our confession is the cause of our salvation. . . . True faith
ought to kindle the heart with zeal for God's glory in
such a way that it pours forth its own flame. And certainly
those who are justified are already in possession of salvation, and therefore believe as much with the heart unto
salvation as make confession with the mouth. Paul, we
see, has made a distinction in such a way as to refer the
cause of justification to faith and also to show what is
required to complete salvation. No one can believe with
the heart without confessing with the mouth. There is
laid on us as a perpetual consequence of faith the necessity of confession with the mouth, but this is not to
ascribe salvation to confession.

JOHN CALVIN

FAITH AND PREACHING

ACTS 16:31 NIV
*They replied, "Believe in the Lord Jesus,
and you will be saved—you and your household."*

This definition of salvation, that one is to believe in Christ, is short and meagre in appearance, but yet it is ample. For Christ alone has all the elements of blessedness and eternal life included in Himself. He offers them to us through the Gospel, but we receive them by faith . . . But the sentence which Luke adds immediately after gives a better description of the nature of faith. Paul and Silas tell the keeper of the prison to believe on the Son of God. Do they come to a stop with that one utterance? Of course not, for it follows in Luke's context that they proclaimed the Word of the Lord. Therefore we see that faith is not a trivial or arid opinion about unknown things, but a clear and distinct knowledge of Christ derived from the Gospel. On the other hand, take away the preaching of the Gospel, and no faith will remain.

JOHN W. FRASER

CHRIST ALONE CONQUERS SIN

1 CORINTHIANS 15:54 ESV
When the perishable puts on the imperishable,
and the mortal puts on immortality,
then shall come to pass the saying that is written:
"Death is swallowed up in victory."

You cast your sins from yourself and onto Christ when you firmly believe that his wounds and sufferings are your sins, to be borne and paid for by him, as we read in Isaiah 53[:6], "The Lord has laid on him the iniquity of us all." St. Peter says, "in his body has he borne our sins on the wood of the cross" (I Peter 2:24). St. Paul says, "God has made him a sinner for us, so that through him we would be made just" (II Corinthians 5:21). You must stake everything on these and similar verses. . . . If we allow sin to remain in our conscience and try to deal with it there . . . it will be much too strong for us and will live on forever. But if we behold it resting on Christ and see it overcome by His resurrection, and then boldly believe this, even it is dead and nullified. Sin cannot remain on Christ, since it is swallowed up by His resurrection.

MARTIN LUTHER

JESUS IS THE SAVIOR WE NEED

LUKE 19:10 NIV
*"For the Son of Man came to seek
and to save what was lost."*

I am a sinner lost and ruined, but I rejoice, for Jesus has come to seek and to save that which was lost. My sins trouble me, but he shall save his people from their sins. Satan annoys me, but he has come to destroy the works of the devil. He is not a nominal, but a real Savior. . . . If a man is called a builder, we expect him to build; if a merchant, we expect him to trade; and as Jesus is a Savior, he will carry on his sacred business, he will save multitudes. Why, surely there is comfortable hope here. Do you not see the dawning in the name of Savior? Surely if he comes to save, and you need saving, there is a blessed suitability in you for one another. A prisoner at the bar is glad to meet one who is by profession an advocate . . . and so a sinner should rejoice at the bare mention of a Savior.

C. H. SPURGEON

GOD OF THE OUTCAST

MATTHEW 9:12-13 NLT
*When he heard this, Jesus replied, "Healthy people
don't need a doctor—sick people do." Then he added,
". . . For I have come to call sinners, not those
who think they are already good enough."*

There is nothing that might be called otherworldly about the ministry of Jesus. He scandalized the religious leaders of his day, the prim and proper ones, because he consorted with the social and religious pariahs of his day. . . . He had dared to have dinner with Zaccheus, a tax collector, a collaborator with the Roman oppressor, and had had the temerity to call him the son of Abraham. He had invited another tax collector, Levi, to become one of his special followers. He had gone to dinner in his house, and there, quite horribly, incredibly, he had sat at the table with all the riff-raff of the town . . . He said he had come to find those who were lost. He even said, quite unbelievably, that these prostitutes, these sinners, would precede the religious teachers and leaders into heaven. Jesus revolutionized religion by showing that God was really a disreputable God, a God on the side of the social pariahs. He showed God as one who accepted us sinners unconditionally.

DESMOND TUTU

OUR ONLY HOPE

ROMANS 3:22–24 NIV
This righteousness from God comes through faith
in Jesus Christ to all who believe. There is no difference,
for all have sinned and fall short of the glory of God,
and are justified freely by his grace through
the redemption that came by Christ Jesus.

Your love covers the multitude of my sins. So when I am fully aware of my sin, when before the justice of heaven only wrath is pronounced upon me, then you are the only person to whom I can escape. If I try to cover myself against the guilt of sin and the wrath of heaven, I will be driven to madness and despair. But if I rely on you to cover my sins, I shall find peace and joy. You suffered and died on the cross to shelter us from our guilt, and take upon yourself the wrath that we deserve. Let me rest under you, and may you transform me into your likeness.

SØREN KIERKEGAARD

FULLY FORGIVEN

ROMANS 8:1 NIV
*Therefore, there is now no condemnation
for those who are in Christ Jesus.*

Do you believe God likes you? "Don't you mean, 'loves me'?" you ask. No, *likes* you. . . . If he were to show up in bodily form, do you think he would seek you out? Would you be someone he would enjoy being around?

Isn't it strange how much more comfortable we are with the concept of *love* than with the concept of *like* when it comes to God's feelings toward us? Why do you think that is true? Often the reason lies in the fact that we have not come to grips with the real extent to which God has forgiven us. Consequently, we live with a subtle sense of condemnation. . . .

The truth is, every reason God had for being angry with us was dealt with at Calvary. Our forgiveness is so complete that God is not only free to love us, he can like us as well. . . . You are not condemned. Christ was condemned on your behalf, and now you are free!

CHARLES STANLEY

KNOWING GOD

1 PETER 3:18 NASB
*For Christ also died for sins once for all, the just for
the unjust, so that He might bring us to God.*

To know God, this is eternal life; this is the purpose
for which we are and were created. The destruction
of our God-awareness was the master blow struck by
Satan in the dark day of our transgression.

To give God back to us was the chief work of Christ
in redemption. To impart Himself to us in personal experience is the first purpose of God in salvation. To bring
acute God-awareness is the best help the Spirit brings in
sanctification. All other steps in grace lead up to this.

Were we allowed but one request, we might gain at a
stroke all things else by praying one all-embracing prayer:

Thyself, Lord! Give me Thyself and I can want no
more.

A. W. TOZER

THE POWER BEHIND THE CHURCH

MATTHEW 16:18 NLT
"Now I say to you that you are Peter,
and upon this rock I will build my church,
and all the powers of hell will not conquer it."

It is a simple fact of history that it was the resurrection belief that brought the Church into being; and when the Church swept out from Jerusalem to the conquest of the earth, it was the resurrection message that was the driving power. . . . For no one seriously believes that a spiritual movement like the Church, so indestructible in its nature, so illimitable in its possibilities, so indispensable in its value for the souls of men, could ever have sprung from, or been inspired by, anything which was not utterly and genuinely real. If Christ had not verily risen, the Church which bears his name would have perished long ago; for fierce attacks, social, political, intellectual, have been launched against it down the years. Many a time, indeed, it has seemed doomed and dead, and the gravediggers . . . have been busy at its tomb; but always it has broken the grave and rolled the stone away. Only the fact of the resurrection of Jesus can explain the Church of the living God.

JAMES S. STEWART

ACCEPTED IN CHRIST

1 CORINTHIANS 1:30 NIV
*It is because of him that you are in Christ Jesus,
who has become for us wisdom from God—that is,
our righteousness, holiness and redemption.*

Though sin wars, it shall not reign; and though it breaks our peace, it cannot separate from his love. Nor is it inconsistent with his holiness and perfection, to manifest his favour to such poor defiled creatures . . . for they are not considered as in themselves, but as one with Jesus, to whom they have fled for refuge, and by whom they live a life of faith. They are accepted in the Beloved, they have an Advocate with the Father, who once made an atonement for their sins and ever lives to make intercession for their persons. Though they cannot fulfill the law, he has fulfilled it for them; though the obedience of the members is defiled and imperfect, the obedience of the Head is spotless and complete; and though there is much evil in them, there is something good, the fruit of his own gracious Spirit. They act from a principle of love, they aim at no less than his glory, and their habitual desires are supremely fixed upon himself.

JOHN NEWTON

HE WILL SAVE

MATTHEW 1:21 NIV
*"She will give birth to a son,
and you are to give him the name Jesus,
because he will save his people from their sins."*

Your foes may be numerous as the devils in hell, strong
and wily; but *He will save.* Your temperament may be
as susceptible to temptation as an aspen-leaf is to the
wind; but *He will save.* Your past years, by repeated acts of
indulgence, may have formed habits strong as iron bands;
but *He will save.* Your circumstances and companions may
be most unfavorable to a life of victory; but *He will save.*
Difficulties are nought to Him; the darkness shineth as the
day. . . . Is it not written, without a single hint at limitation or reserve?—"He shall save His people from their
sins." And shall He not do so?

If there be, therefore, perpetual failure in your life, it
cannot arise from any weakness or impotence in the
Mighty God, but from some failure on your part. That
failure may probably be discovered in one of three hiding
places—perfect surrender, deficient faith, or neglected
communion. But when the intention of the soul is right
with God, without doubt *He will save.*

F. B. MEYER

GOD'S PLEASURE IN CHRIST'S SACRIFICE

MATTHEW 20:28 NLT
*"For even I, the Son of Man,
came here not to be served but to serve others,
and to give my life as a ransom for many."*

God was so set, from everlasting, on the salvation of sinners that the most awful steps that had to be taken in order to work out that salvation are here said to have absolutely pleased Him. It is somewhat like our Lord's own words—"I delight to do Thy will": even when His Father's will led Him to the garden of Gethsemane and the Cross of Calvary . . . God could not be pleased with the death of His Son—in itself. No. But nothing has ever pleased Him more than that His Son should lay down His life in atonement for those sinners whom the Father had chosen and ordained to everlasting life.

. . . It pleased the Lord to bruise Him, because in this way alone could God's full hatred of sin be declared to men and angels, and at the same time God's justice might be manifested in the salvation of sinners.

ALEXANDER WHYTE

JESUS IS THE WAY

JOHN 17:23 ESV

*"I in them and you in me, that they may become
perfectly one, so that the world may know that you
sent me and loved them even as you loved me."*

By nature we are strangers, yea, enemies to God; but we are reconciled, brought nigh, and become his children, by faith in Christ Jesus. . . . He is the medium of this inestimable privilege: for he is the way, the only way, of intercourse between heaven and earth; the sinner's way to God, and God's way of mercy to the sinner.

God, if considered abstracted from the revelation of himself in the person of Jesus, is a consuming fire; and if he should look upon us with respect to his covenant of mercy established in the Mediator, we could expect nothing from him but indignation and wrath. But when his Holy Spirit enables us to receive the record which he had given of his Son, we are delivered and secured from condemnation; we are accepted in the Beloved; we are united to him in whom all the fullness of the Godhead substantially dwells, and all the riches of divine wisdom, power, and love, are treasured up.

JOHN NEWTON

FAITH IS THE KEY

HEBREWS 11:6 ESV
And without faith it is impossible to please him, for whoever would draw near to God must believe that he exists and that he rewards those who seek him.

Apart from faith neither Enoch nor anyone else could ever have been pleasing to God. The faith which our author has in mind embraces belief in the invisible spiritual order and belief in the promises of God which have not yet been fulfilled. Belief in the invisible spiritual order involves, first and foremost, belief in Him who is "King of the ages, immortal, invisible, the only God" (I Timothy 1:17); and belief in God carries with it necessarily belief in His word. . . . Those who approach Him can do so in full confidence that He exists, that His word is true, and that He will never put off or disappoint the soul that sincerely seeks Him. For all that He has revealed of Himself, whether through the prophets or in His Son, assures us that He is altogether worthy of His people's trust.

The reward desired by those who seek Him is the joy of finding Him: He Himself proves to be their "exceeding joy" (Psalm 43:4).

F. F. BRUCE

JESUS, MY ALL

MATTHEW 18:11 NKJV
*"For the Son of Man has come to save
that which was lost."*

Lord, at Thy mercy seat, humbly I fall;
Pleading Thy promise sweet, Lord, hear my call;
Now let Thy work begin; oh, make me pure within,
Cleanse me from every sin, Jesus, my all.

Tears of repentant grief silently fall;
Help Thou my unbelief; hear Thou my call;
Oh, how I pine for Thee! 'Tis all my hope and plea:
Jesus has died for me, Jesus, my all.

Still at Thy mercy seat, Savior, I fall;
Trusting Thy promise sweet, heard is my call;
Faith wings my soul to Thee; this all my song shall be,
Jesus has died for me, Jesus, my all.

FANNY CROSBY

FAITH IN CHRIST

ROMANS 3:22 NIT

*We are made right in God's sight when we trust
in Jesus Christ to take away our sins. And we all
can be saved in this same way, no matter
who we are or what we have done.*

How can man once again be accepted in God's eyes?
By his faith in Jesus Christ. Whether you see it yet
or not, that is good. That means I can't work for it. Where
I have gone wrong, God can forgive me. If I place my
faith into what Jesus Christ has done, that is the basis of
my being acceptable in God's eyes. That is good news.
God says, "I have done it for you in the Lord Jesus. You
place your faith into My Son. I accept you on the basis of
what He has done, not on the basis of what you can do
for Him. It is through faith in Jesus Christ."

Faith is not based on what I think He will do for me.
My faith is based on what He has already done for me.
That has to be the bottom line of our faith. . . . It is to
put everything, rest everything based on that which Jesus
Christ has done for you and me.

WAYNE BARBER

BOASTING IN THE CROSS

GALATIANS 6:14 ESV
*But far be it from me to boast except in the cross
of our Lord Jesus Christ, by which the world
has been crucified to me, and I to the world.*

Truly the symbol of the cross is considered despicable according to the world and among people. But in heaven and among the faithful, it is the highest glory. Poverty, too, is seen as despicable, but we boast in it. It is cheapened by the public and they laugh at it, but we are elated by it. In the same way, we boast in the cross. . . .

But what is boasting in the cross? Boasting in the fact that Christ took on the form of a slave for my sake and suffered for me when I was the slave, the enemy, the unfeeling one. He loved me so much that He gave Himself over to a curse for me. What can compare to this? If servants only receive praise from their masters, who they are bound to kin by nature, and are elated by it, how much more must we boast when our Master, God Himself, isn't ashamed of the cross Christ endured for us.

CHRYSOSTOM

ABOUT
HIMSELF

---

*I count all things to be loss in view
of the surpassing value of knowing
Christ Jesus my Lord.*

PHILIPPIANS 3:8 NASB

ABOUT HIMSELF

God's word declares His character. His claims and abilities are never uncertain or tentative. God never tries; He does. Because He speaks from beyond His time-bound creation, His promises are not so much statements about the future as they are statements of fact. We might have to wait for one of God's promises to be fulfilled, but as far as their certainty, they are complete when God makes them. He dwells where promise and fulfillment occur simultaneously.

While we tend to think of God's promises as statements about His actions, they are, in a deeper way, statements about who He is. Through His promises we not only know what God will do, we also get to know God. We discover that we can't trust His promises until we learn to trust Him. And the more we learn to trust Him, the more we see His promises as delightful confirmations of God's trustworthiness rather than as reasons to trust. God's promises usher us into knowing God.

ENCOUNTERING JESUS

PSALM 34:8 NASB
O taste and see that the LORD is good.

Once, as I rode out into the woods for my health, in 1737, having alighted from my horse in a retired place . . . I had a view that for me was extraordinary, of the glory of the Son of God, as Mediator between God and man, and his wonderful, great, full, pure and sweet grace and love, and meek and gentle condescension. This grace that appeared so calm and sweet, appeared also great above the heavens. The person of Christ appeared ineffably excellent with an excellency great enough to swallow up all thought and conception . which continued as near as I can judge, about an hour; which kept me the greater part of the time in a flood of tears, and weeping aloud. I felt an ardency of soul to be, what I know not otherwise how to express, emptied and annihilated; to lie in the dust, and to be full of Christ alone; to love him with a holy and pure love; to trust in him; to live upon him; to serve and follow him; and to be perfectly sanctified and made pure, with a divine and heavenly purity.

JONATHAN EDWARDS

DELIGHTING IN GOD

1 TIMOTHY 1:17 ESV

*To the King of ages, immortal, invisible, the only God,
be honor and glory forever and ever. Amen.*

The first instance that I remember of that sort of inward, sweet delight in God and divine things that I have lived much in since, was on reading those words, 1 Timothy 1:17. As I read the words, there came into my soul, and was as it were diffused through it, a sense of the glory of the Divine Being; a new sense, quite different from any thing I ever experienced before. I thought with myself, how excellent a Being that was, and how happy I should be, if I might enjoy that God, and be rapt up to him in heaven, and be as it were swallowed up in him for ever! I kept saying, and as it were singing over these words of scripture to myself, and went to pray to God that I might enjoy him. . . .

From about that time, I began to have a new kind of apprehensions and ideas of Christ, and the work of redemption, and the glorious way of salvation by him. . . . And my mind was greatly engaged to spend my time in reading and meditating on Christ, on the beauty and excellency of his person.

JONATHAN EDWARDS

PARTAKERS OF HIS HOLINESS

ISAIAH 6:2–3 ESV

*Above him stood the seraphim. . . . And one called
to another and said: "Holy, holy, holy is the LORD
of hosts; the whole earth is full of his glory!"*

Before the uncreated fire of God's holiness, angels veil
their faces. Yea, the heavens are not clean, and the
stars are not pure in His sight. No honest man can say "I
am holy," but neither is any honest man willing to ignore
the solemn words of the inspired writer, "Follow peace
with all men, and holiness, without which no man shall
see the Lord."

Caught in this dilemma, what are we Christians to do?
We must, like Moses, cover ourselves with faith and
humility while we steal a quick look at the God whom
no man can see and live. The broken and the contrite
heart He will not despise. We must hide our unholiness
in the wounds of Christ as Moses hid himself in the cleft
of the rock while the glory of God passed by. We must
take refuge from God in God. Above all we must believe
that God sees us perfect in His Son while He disciplines
and chastens and purges us that we may be partakers of
His holiness.

A. W. TOZER

THE FULLNESS OF CHRIST

ISAIAH 6:3 NLT
*In a great chorus they sang, "Holy, holy, holy
is the LORD Almighty! The whole earth is filled
with his glory!"*

O God, . . .
  Help me to delight more in what I receive
    from Christ,
  more in that fullness which is in him,
  the fountain of all his glory.
Let me not think to receive the Spirit from him as a
    "thing"
  apart from finding, drinking, being filled with him.
To this end, O God,
  do thou establish me in Christ,
  settle me, give me a being there,
  assure me with certainty that all this is mine,
  for this only will fill my heart with joy and peace.

UNKNOWN

THE GREATNESS OF GOD

JEREMIAH 32:17 NLT

O Sovereign LORD! You have made the heavens and earth by your great power. Nothing is too hard for you!

Now I want you to take special notice of the words written in Jeremiah 32:17: "Ah Lord God! behold, thou hast made the heaven and the earth by thy great power and stretched-out arm, and there is nothing too hard for thee."

I think the Lord was pleased with this prayer of Jeremiah, for he responds to him in the twenty-seventh verse:

"Behold, I am the Lord, the God of all flesh: is there any thing too hard for me?" God likes to have his people believe that there is nothing too hard for him. We talk about Frederick the Great, and Alexander the Great, but how very little are these mighty men when we come to compare them with God. If Tyndall, or Huxley, or Darwin had ever created any light, what a sound of trumpets there would have been about it! but we read in the Bible the very simple statement, "And God said, Let there be light: and there was light,"—and that is all there is said about it.

DWIGHT L. MOODY

THE WORK OF CHRIST

JOHN 4:14 ESV
"But whoever drinks of the water that I will give him
will never be thirsty forever. The water that
I will give him will become in him
a spring of water welling up to eternal life."

Faith is believing that Christ is what He is said to be and that He will do what He has promised to do, and then to expect this of Him. The Scriptures speak of Jesus Christ as being God in human flesh, as being perfect in His character, as being made a sin offering on our behalf, as bearing our sins in His own body on the tree. The Scripture speaks of Him as having finished transgression, made an end of sin, and brought in everlasting righteousness. The sacred records further tell us that He "rose again" (1 Corinthians 15:4) from the dead, that He "ever liveth to make intercession for us" (Hebrews 7:25), that He has gone up into glory and has taken possession of heaven on the behalf of His people, and that He will shortly come again "to judge the . . . world with righteousness, and the peoples with equity" (Psalm 98:9 ASV).

C. H. SPURGEON

LIVING WATER

JOHN 7:37–38 NIV
*On the last and greatest day of the Feast, Jesus stood
and said in a loud voice, "If anyone is thirsty,
let him come to me and drink. Whoever believes in me,
as the Scripture has said, streams of living water
will flow from within him."*

The springs of living water concept in John 7 is actually a compilation of metaphors. Each element in the total picture makes its own contribution to the spiritual and psychological impact Jesus was promising his hearers. Also, each element seems to speak to a different group of people. To the hardened unbeliever Jesus says, "I see right through your exterior shell; inside you are on a haunting search." To those who know they are thirsty—the seekers—he says, "Do not look for signs; be prepared to receive the quiet water I am offering to you." To the new believer he says, "My living water will give you life, life which will never thirst again." And to the more mature believer, Jesus says, "My work in your life will result in great blessing to others and out of you will flow the over-abundance of my goodness to you."

What a divinely inspired solution to the mire of narcissism in which we find ourselves!

JAMES R. BECK

CHRIST IS ALL

JOHN 8:58 NLT
*Jesus answered, "The truth is, I existed
before Abraham was even born!"*

The Gospel of John is the most profound of all the
Gospels, as well as being the last written. In it we are
shown what is God's estimate of Christ. So we are made
to understand that it is not a matter of God requiring a
lamb, giving his people bread, or providing us with a way,
nor even that Christ can use his power to restore a dead
man's life or a blind man's sight. In the whole of this
Gospel we are confronted with one monumental fact,
which is that Christ is all these things.

He did not say that he is able to give people light, but
rather that he himself is the Light of the world. He did
not only promise us the bread of life, but assured us that
he himself is the Bread of life. He did not just say that he
would guide us in the way, but insisted that he himself is
the Way. In Christianity Christ is everything. What he
gives is his very own Self.

WATCHMAN NEE

THE DEITY OF CHRIST

COLOSSIANS 1:15 NASB
He is the image of the invisible God,
the firstborn of all creation.

Billy Graham is careful that the full message of the incarnate Christ be declared and understood. He writes, "It is actually the deity of Christ that above anything else gives to Christianity its sanction, authority, power and its meaning."

When Billy was preaching in Nagaland, in northeast India, where many in the congregation were from Hindu, Muslim, or syncretistic backgrounds, he took great care to emphasize that the God he proclaimed was not "one of the gods," but *"the* God." This did not prove acceptable to everyone attending given their diverse religious orientations, but in the three days the evangelist preached there, more than four thousand people made a decision for Christ.

In his well-known book *The Secret of Happiness*, Graham expresses the concept of the deity of Jesus quite pointedly: "Jesus was not only man, but he was God himself, come down from the glory of heaven to walk on earth and show us what God is like. Christ is 'the image of the invisible God'" (Colossians 1:15).

LEWIS DRUMMOND

THE LOVE OF GOD

PSALM 103:13 NLT
The LORD is like a father to his children,
tender and compassionate to those who fear him.

Don't measure God's mind by your own. It would be a poor love that depended not on itself, but on the feelings of the person loved. A crying baby turns away from its mother's breast, but she does not put it away till it stops crying. She holds it closer. For my part, in the worst mood I am ever in, when I don't feel I love God at all, I just look up to His love. I say to Him, "Look at me. See what state I am in. Help me!" Ah! you would wonder how that makes peace. And the love comes of itself; sometimes so strong, it nearly breaks my heart.

GEORGE MACDONALD

THE RESURRECTION AND THE LIFE

JOHN 11:25 NKJV

Jesus said to her, "I am the resurrection and the life.
He who believes in Me, though he may die,
he shall live."

What should be the Christian's attitude to death? It is still an enemy, unnatural, unpleasant and undignified—in fact "the last enemy to be destroyed." Yet, it is a defeated enemy—Christ has taken away our sins, death has lost its power to harm and therefore to terrify. Jesus summed it up in one of his greatest affirmations: "I am the resurrection and the life. He who believes in me will live, even though he dies; and whoever lives and believes in me will never die" (John. 11:25–26). That is, Jesus is the resurrection of believers who die, and the believers who live. His promise to the former is "you will live," meaning not just that you will survive, but that you will be resurrected. His promise to the latter is "you will never die," meaning not that you will escape death, but that death will prove to be a trivial episode, a transition to fullness of life.

JOHN STOTT

ABIDE IN ME

JOHN 15:5 NIV
"I am the vine; you are the branches.
If a man remains in me and I in him,
he will bear much fruit; apart from me
you can do nothing."

It is when we try to understand the meaning of the parable that the blessed command reveals its true power. The thought of what the vine is to the branch, and Jesus to the believer, will give new force to the words, "Abide in Me."

It will be as if He says, "Think, soul, how completely I belong to you. I have joined Myself inseparably to you; all the fullness and fatness of the Vine are yours. Abide in Me. You are weak, but I am strong; you are poor, but I am rich. Only abide in Me; yield yourself wholly to My teaching and rule; . . . Abide in Me."

Shall I hesitate, or withhold consent? Shall I not begin to look upon it as the most blessed and joyful thing under heaven? On my part, abiding is nothing but the acceptance of my position, . . . the surrender of faith to the strong Vine to hold the feeble branch.

Yes, I will, I do abide in You, blessed Lord Jesus.

ANDREW MURRAY

BREAD OF LIFE

JOHN 6:35 ESV
Jesus said to them, "I am the bread of life;
whoever comes to me shall not hunger,
and whoever believes in me shall never thirst."

When we eat bread for the nourishment of the body, both our own weakness and the power of divine grace are more apparent than if God were to impart a secret power to nourish the body without food. Thus the analogy from the body to the soul makes Christ's grace more clearly perceptible. For when we hear that Christ is the bread by which our souls must be fed, it sinks deeper into our minds than if Christ had simply said that He is our life. . . .

But the eating is the effect and fruit of faith rather than faith itself. For faith does not look at Christ merely from afar, but embraces Him, that He may become ours and dwell in us. It causes us to be united in His body, to have life in common with Him and, in short, to be one with Him. It is therefore true that we eat Christ by faith alone, so long as we grasp how faith unites us to him.

T. H. L. PARKER

CHRIST IS REVEALED IN WORDS

JOHN 14:8–9 ESV

Philip said to him, "Lord, show us the Father, and it is enough for us." Jesus said to him, "Have I been with you so long, and you still do not know me, Philip? Whoever has seen me has seen the Father."

Some today argue as if revelation in the person of Christ takes us beyond the realm of verbal revelation altogether. But our author does not think so; rather, he regards verbal revelation as of the essence of our Lord's own revelatory ministry. This appears from his reference in Hebrews 2:3 to the "great salvation" which "having at the first been *spoken* through the Lord, was confirmed unto us by them that *heard* him. . . ."

Accordingly, at the end of the letter to the Hebrews, having referred to the "voice of words" which Israel heard at Sinai (12:19), the writer sums up his appeal thus: "See that ye refuse not him that *speaketh*. For if they escaped not, When they refused him that *warned* them upon earth, much more shall not we escape, who turn away from him that *warneth* from heaven: Whose voice then shook the earth: but now he hath *promised, saying,* yet once more will I make to tremble not the earth only, but also the heaven" (12:25f., citing Haggai 2:6).

J. I. PACKER

THE RESURRECTION AND THE LIFE

JOHN 11:25 NLT

*Jesus told her, "I am the resurrection and the life.
Those who believe in me, even though they die
like everyone else, will live again."*

Christ first proclaims that He is the resurrection and the life. Then He explains each clause of the statement separately and distinctly First, He calls Himself the resurrection; for restoration from death to life precedes the state of life. But the whole human race is plunged in death. Therefore, no man will possess life unless he is first risen from the dead. Hence Christ teaches that He is the beginning of life. . . .

The explanation which follows shows plainly that He is speaking of spiritual life: "He that believeth on me, though he die, yet shall he live." In what way, then, is Christ the resurrection? In that by His Spirit He regenerates the sons of Adam, who by their sin were alienated from God, so that they begin to live a new life.

. . . Therefore those who believe in Christ, although they had before been dead, begin to live; for faith is a spiritual resurrection of the soul, and as it were quickens the soul, that it may live unto God.

JOHN CALVIN

THE SEARCHER OF HEARTS

ISAIAH 53:5 NIV

But he was pierced for our transgressions, he was crushed for our iniquities; the punishment that brought us peace was upon him, and by his wounds we are healed.

Jesus Christ is the supreme Sacrifice for the sin of the world; He is "the Lamb of God, which taketh away the sin of the world!" How the Death of Jesus looms all through the Bible! It is through His death that we are made partakers of His life and can have gifted to us a pure heart, which He says is the condition for seeing God.

... The Lamb is not only the supreme Sacrifice for man's sin, He is the Searcher of hearts, searching to the inmost recesses of mind and motive. It is not a curious searching, not an uncanny searching, but the deep wholesome searching the Holy Spirit gives in order to convict men of their sin and need of a Saviour; then when they come to the Cross, and through it accept deliverance from sin, Jesus Christ becomes the Sovereign of their lives; they love Him personally and passionately beyond all other loves of earth.

OSWALD CHAMBERS

THE POWER OF GOD'S NAME

PSALM 86:9 NIV
All the nations you have made
will come and worship before you, O Lord;
they will bring glory to your name.

Hallowed be Thy Name." Oh, that all the earth would ever reverence it. As for ourselves, enable us by Thy grace to use it with awe and trembling; and may a consideration of the glorious character which is intended by Thy gracious name, ever lay us in the very dust before Thee, and yet lift us up with holy joy and with an unwavering confidence.

Glorious Jehovah, the God of Abraham, of Isaac, and of Jacob, Thou hast not changed: Thou art still a covenant God, and Thou keepest that covenant to all Thy people . . . All Thy promises are yea and amen in Christ Jesus to Thy glory by us, and we believe those promises will be fulfilled in every jot and tittle: not one of them shall want its mate, not one of them shall fall to the ground like the frivolous words of men. Hast Thou said and wilt Thou not do it? Hast Thou commanded and shall it not come to pass?

C. H. SPURGEON

THIRSTING FOR GOD

PSALM 42:2 ESV
My soul thirsts for God, for the living God.
When shall I come and appear before God?

No man is made to be satisfied from himself. For the stilling of our own hearts, for the satisfying of our own nature, for strengthening and joy of our being, we need to go beyond ourselves, and to fix upon something external to ourselves. . . . If a man's life is to be strong and happy, he must get the foundation of his strength somewhere else than in his own soul. . . .

We are made, next, to need, not *things,* but *living beings.* "My soul thirsteth"—for what? An abstraction, a possession, riches, a thing? No! "my soul thirsteth for God, for *the living God.*" Yes, hearts want hearts. The converse of Christ's saying is equally true; He said, "God is a Spirit, and they that worship Him must worship Him in spirit"; man has a spirit, and must have Spirit to worship, to lean upon, to live by, or be inefficient and unsatisfactory. Oh, lay this to heart, my brother!—no *things* can satisfy a living soul.

ALEXANDER MACLAREN

OUR GREAT GOD

JOHN 8:58 NIV
*"I tell you the truth," Jesus answered,
"before Abraham was born, I am!"*

When we say "Jehovah!" "Lord!" what we ought to mean is this, that we are gazing upon the majestic, glorious thought of Being, self-derived, self-motivated, self-ruled, the being of Him whose Name can only be, "I am that I am." . . . And this infinite, changeless Rock is laid for our confidence, Jehovah the Eternal, the Self-subsisting, Self-sufficing One.

There is more than that thought in this wondrous Name, for it not only expresses the timeless, unlimited, and changeless being of God, but also the truth that He has entered into what He deigns to call a Covenant with us men. The name Jehovah is the seal of that ancient Covenant, and God has thereby bound Himself to us by promises that cannot be abrogated. So that when we say, "O Lord!" we summon up before ourselves, and grasp as the grounds of our confidence, and we humbly present before Him as the motives, if we may so call them, for His action, His own infinite being, and His covenanted grace.

ALEXANDER MACLAREN

HOLY, HOLY, HOLY

ISAIAH 6:3-4 NIV

And they were calling to one another: "Holy, holy, holy is the Lord Almighty; the whole earth is full of his glory." At the sound of their voices the doorposts and thresholds shook and the temple was filled with smoke.

What the reader felt in the description of the attitude of the heavenly beings is confirmed for him by their song of praise which celebrates the king Yahweh Sabaoth as the one holy one. The threefold repetition of the 'holy' characterizes him as the all-holy and sole-holy one. The refrain in Psalm 99:3, 5, 9 seems to be almost in concentrated form here. From the holiness of God there goes out to mankind the call to be holy themselves (Leviticus 19:2). Because God is other than all the world, those who belong to him are also to correspond to him in their purity and righteousness. This God, who is designated "the Holy One of Israel" especially in the book of Isaiah, is here given his cult-name Yahweh Sebaoth, which at the latest arose in the Jerusalem temple. At all events, this name stresses the unlimited power of Yahweh over all heavenly and earthly authorities.

OTTO KAIZER

JESUS IS THE WAY TO GOD

JOHN 14:6 NLT
*Jesus told him, "I am the way,
the truth, and the life.
No one can come to the Father
except through me."*

If Jesus Christ was God He must say that He is the way, the truth and the life, or words of equivalent meaning, and we find He adds as a matter of unalterable fact that no one comes into contact with God except through Him. This is the third empirical test. Do people in fact know God except through Christ? . . . It is very significant that those who reject Christ's claim as fantastic, or even ignore it, *do not know God;* whereas many simple people with little theology or philosophy do find that they "know God" when they give their confidence to the Character that they can trust and love. . . .

It is therefore clear that to accept the claim of Christ after proper and careful thought is not entirely a leap into the dark. For the very decision will, as thousands have proved, carry with it an incontrovertible inner endorsement that is worth any amount of argument.

J. B. PHILLIPS

THE VINE AND THE VINEGROWER

JOHN 15:1 NRSV
*"I am the true vine,
and my Father is the vinegrower."*

I am," he says, "the true vine, and my Father is the cultivator. Every branch in me not bearing fruit he will take away; and every one that bears fruit he will trim clean, that it may bring forth even more fruit." Surely the cultivator and the vine are not one thing? Therefore Christ is the vine in that regard in which he said, "The Father is greater than I." But in the regard in which he said, "I and the Father, we are one thing," he himself too is the cultivator. And he is not such as are they who exercise their ministry by working from without; but he is such that he also gives growth from within. For "neither he who plants is anything, nor he who waters, but God who gives the growth." But certainly Christ is God; for the Word was God, and because of this he and the Father are one thing. And if the Word was made flesh, which he was not, he remains what he was.

AUGUSTINE

KING OF KINGS

MARK 15:2 NLT

Pilate asked Jesus, "Are you the King of the Jews?"
Jesus replied, "Yes, it is as you say."

There is still time—even now this morning—when you can accept the amnesty that King Jesus holds out to you, and renounce your allegiance to self and success and money and family and physical pleasure and security—and whatever else rules you more than Jesus. And you can bow and receive Christ as your King and swear allegiance to him, and be on his side with everlasting joy. . . .

Jesus came the first time, and he is coming again, as the king over all kings. King of Israel, king of all the nations, king of nature and the universe. Until he comes again, there is a day of amnesty and forgiveness and patience. He still rides a donkey and not yet a white war-horse with a rod of iron. He is ready to save all who receive him as Savior and Treasure and King. Come to him. Know him. Receive him. Live your life in allegiance to him.

JOHN PIPER

STAY CLOSE TO THE SHEPHERD

HEBREWS 13:20–21 NASB

*Now the God of peace, who brought up from the dead
the great Shepherd of the sheep through the blood of
the eternal covenant, even Jesus our Lord, equip you in
every good thing to do His will, working in us that
which is pleasing in His sight, through Jesus Christ,
to whom be the glory forever and ever. Amen.*

It is an old saying, "The sheep that keeps nearest the
shepherd gets the most salt."

One summer I went up on to the mountain with my
brother, who was going to salt his sheep; and I noticed
one sheep which came right up to him, and stood by
him, and got all the salt it wanted; then it put its nose into
his pocket and got an apple; but all the other sheep
seemed a little afraid of him. I asked him how it was, and
he said. "That sheep has been brought up a cosset, and
isn't a bit afraid of me." So it is with those Christians who
keep close to Christ; they are like the sheep that gets the
most salt; but a good many Christians seem a little afraid
of the Shepherd; and because they are afraid and keep
away from him, they never get much salt.

DWIGHT L. MOODY

THE GOOD SHEPHERD

JOHN 10:11 ESV
"I am the good shepherd.
The good shepherd lays down his life for the sheep."

From His unique love for the sheep, He shows that He really acts as a shepherd towards them, for He is so anxious for their salvation that He does not even spare His own life. . . . What Augustine says is very true, that we are here shown what we should desire, and what avoid, and what endure, in the government of the Church. Nothing is more to be wished than that the Church should be governed by good and diligent shepherds. Christ says that He is the one good Shepherd, who keeps His Church safe and sound, by Himself in the first place, and then also by His instruments: whenever there is good order and fit men rule, Christ acts as the Shepherd in fact. But there are many wolves and thieves who, under the mask of shepherds, wickedly scatter the Church. Christ denounces them as men to be avoided, whatever name they may assume.

JOHN CALVIN

THE LIGHT OF THE WORLD

JOHN 8:12 NLT

*Jesus said to the people, "I am the light of the world.
If you follow me, you won't be stumbling through
the darkness, because you will have
the light that leads to life."*

The first statement and declaration must be the greatest heresy. When Christ states: "I am the Light of the world," they say: "What presumption, to say that You are the Light of the whole world!" This implies: "Darkness rules wherever I am not; whenever I am extinguished, no one sees anything." What becomes of Moses and all other teachers and doctors when He says: "It is I"? . . . If He had only been more moderate and reasonable and had said: "I am the Light of this country, of this kingdom, of this house, of this nation, of this temple," it might have been accepted as a fair claim. But to come out boastfully and take in the entire world in one bite, to speak so disparagingly and casually of the world, to say that it dwells in sheer darkness without Him—that is an arrogant claim, that is bidding everyone else be silent, that is calling all wise people fools.

MARTIN LUTHER

DAY 105

INFINITE HEIGHT, INFINITE LOVE

REVELATION 5:5–6 NIV
*Then one of the elders said to me, "Do not weep!
See, the Lion of the tribe of Judah, the Root of David,
has triumphed. He is able to open the scroll and
its seven seals." Then I saw a Lamb, looking as if it
had been slain, standing in the center of the throne,
encircled by the four living creatures and the elders.
He had seven horns and seven eyes, which are
the seven spirits of God sent out into all the earth.*

There do meet in Jesus Christ infinite highness and infinite condescension. Christ, as he is God, is infinitely great and high above all. He is higher than the kings of the earth, for he is King of kings, and Lord of lords. . . .

And yet he is one of infinite condescension. None are so low or inferior, but Christ's condescension is sufficient to take a gracious notice of them. . . .

His condescension is great enough to become their friend, to become their companion, to unite their souls to him in spiritual marriage. It is enough to take their nature upon him, to become one of them, that he may be one with them. Yea, it is great enough to abase himself yet lower for them, even to expose himself to shame and spitting; yea, to yield up himself to an ignominious death for them.

JONATHAN EDWARDS

COMMUNITY IN CHRIST

1 TIMOTHY 2:5 NLT

*For there is only one God and one Mediator who can
reconcile God and people. He is the man Christ Jesus.*

When God's Son took on flesh, he truly and bodily
took on, out of pure grace, our being, our nature,
ourselves. This was the eternal counsel of the triune God.
Now we are in him. Where he is, there we are too, in the
incarnation, on the Cross, and in his resurrection. We
belong to him because we are in him. That is why the
Scriptures call us the Body of Christ.

But if, before we could know and wish it, we have
been chosen and accepted with the whole Church in
Jesus Christ, then we also belong to him in eternity *with*
one another. We who live here in fellowship with him
will one day be with him in eternal fellowship.

He who looks upon his brother should know that he
will be eternally united with him in Jesus Christ. Christian community means community in and through Jesus
Christ. On this presupposition rests everything that the
Scriptures provide in the way of directions and precepts
for the communal life of Christians.

DIETRICH BONHOEFFER

ABOUT
FORGIVENESS

He is so rich in kindness that he purchased our freedom through the blood of his Son, and our sins are forgiven.

EPHESIANS 1:7 NLT

ABOUT FORGIVENESS

The prelude to forgiveness isn't "I'm sorry." That's only an admission of "wrongfeeling," not wrongdoing. Saying "I'm sorry" doesn't expect (or even allow) the offended party to respond. We access (or are denied) forgiveness when we admit, "I was wrong. Will you forgive me?" We, the offenders, are naturally terrified of this approach. It makes us vulnerable to the one we have offended. Our request gives the one we have hurt the opportunity to say, "No, I won't forgive you." Unless we are willing to face that danger, we probably don't really want to be forgiven.

God promises forgiveness. Jesus went out of His way to demonstrate God's eagerness to forgive (see Mark 2:10). He has declared Himself "faithful and just to forgive us our sins" (see 1 John 1:9). Our problem isn't God's assurance of forgiveness but our tendency to take that forgiveness lightly. As you meditate with the following reflections on God's promised forgiveness, consider how much you value hearing God say, "Yes, I forgive you."

NO CONDEMNATION

ROMANS 8:1 NKJV

*There is therefore now no condemnation to those who
are in Christ Jesus, who do not walk according
to the flesh, but according to the Spirit.*

It is of all importance that we realize that we do not
stand before God on the ground of responsibility. The
responsible man failed utterly to keep his obligations.
There was nothing for him, therefore, but condemnation,
but our Lord Jesus Christ has borne that condemnation;
He voluntarily, in infinite grace, took the place of the
sinner and bore his judgment upon the cross. Now in resurrection, as we have seen, all who believe are not only
given a perfect representation by Him before the throne
of God, but we are in Him in virtue of being partakers of
His life.

It is when the soul enters into this experimentally, real-
izing that the death of Christ, in which faith has given
him part, has severed the link that bound him to the
world and all its purposes and has freed him from all
necessity to be subject to sin in the flesh, that he will be
free to glorify God as he walks in newness of life.

H. A. IRONSIDE

THE PRINCIPLE OF FORGIVENESS

JOHN 1:29 NIV

*The next day John saw Jesus coming toward him
and said, "Look, the Lamb of God,
who takes away the sin of the world!"*

Fortunately, the message of John does not stop with baptism and repentance. It isn't complete without the third, most joyous element, forgiveness. And in the teachings of Jesus, and in his life, death, and resurrection, the principle of forgiveness comes to complete fruition. It is important not to wallow in guilt or embarrassment but to wipe the slate clean, turn away from the past, and fully accept the good news of Christ's complete and total forgiveness. We couldn't confess without the assurance of forgiveness. If self-examination brings us the sorrow and shame of recognizing our sinfulness, then accepting God's mercy, promised to us by Christ, makes possible a new life of peace, joy, and adventure. No longer uneasy about our past failings, we can concentrate today and tomorrow on a closer walk with God and our fellow human beings.

JIMMY CARTER

THE SACRIFICE OF CHRIST

EPHESIANS 5:1–2 NRSV

*Therefore be imitators of God, as beloved children,
and live in love, as Christ loved us and gave himself
up for us, a fragrant offering and sacrifice to God.*

The scriptures also teach the absolute *necessity* of the atonement of Christ, and that we can obtain forgiveness and salvation through that only. The sacrifices appointed to be made by the ancient Israelites seem evidently to point to Christ and to show the necessity of the vicarious sacrifice of him, who is therefore said to be "our *passover sacrificed* for us;" and to have "given himself for us, an *offering* and *a sacrifice* to God, for a sweet smelling savor;" and "now once in the end of the world, to have appeared, to put away sin, by the *sacrifice* of himself" (1 Corinthians 5:7, Ephesians 5:2, Hebrews 9:26). As the ancient Israelites could obtain pardon in no other way than by those sacrifices, this teaches us that we can obtain it only by the sacrifice of Christ.

JONATHAN EDWARDS

THE THIRST FOR FORGIVENESS

LUKE 18:13–14 ESV

*"But the tax collector, standing far off, would not even
lift up his eyes to heaven, but beat his breast,
saying, 'God, be merciful to me, a sinner!' I tell you,
this man went down to his house justified."*

There is no thirst of the soul so consuming as the desire for pardon. The sense of its bestowal is the starting-point of all goodness. It comes bringing with it, if not the freshness of innocence, yet a glow of inspiration that nerves feeble hands for hard tasks, a fire of hope that lights anew the old high ideal, so that it stands before the eye in clear relief, beckoning us to make it our own. To be able to look into God's face, and know with the knowledge of faith that there is nothing between the soul and Him, is to experience the fullest peace the soul can know. Whatever else pardon may be, it is above all things admission into full fellowship with God.

CHARLES H. BRENT

CHRIST CONQUERS SIN AND DEATH

JOHN 3:36 NIV

*"Whoever believes in the Son has eternal life,
but whoever rejects the Son will not see life,
for God's wrath remains on him."*

Thus the Christian (if he but believes it) may glory in the merits of Christ and in all his blessings as though he himself had won them. . . . Let Christians thus say in full confidence, "O death, where is your victory? O death, where is your sting?" namely, sin. "The sting of death is sin, and the strength of sin is the law. But thanks be to God who gave us the victory through Jesus Christ, our Lord" (1 Corinthians 15:55–57). That is to say, the law makes us sinners and sin makes us guilty of death. Who has conquered these two? Was it our righteousness? Was it our life? No, it was Jesus Christ, rising from death, condemning sin and death, imparting his righteousness to us, bestowing his merits on us, and holding his hand over us. Now all is well with us; we fulfil the law and vanquish sin and death. For all of this let there be honor, praise, and thanksgiving to God for ever and ever. Amen.

MARTIN LUTHER

VICTORY OVER SIN

1 JOHN 1:8–9 NLT
If we say we have no sin, we are only fooling
ourselves and refusing to accept the truth.
But if we confess our sins to him,
he is faithful and just to forgive us and
to cleanse us from every wrong.

Are you tempted to do some wrong at this moment? If you are, remember that Jesus rose from the dead, remember that at this moment He is living at the right hand of God in the glory; remember that He has all power in heaven and on earth, and that, therefore, He can give you victory right now. Believe what God tells you in His Word, that Jesus has power to save you this moment "to the uttermost" (Hebrews 7:25). Believe that He has power to give you victory over this sin that now besets you. Ask Him to give you victory; expect Him to do it. in this way, by looking unto the risen Christ for victory, you may have victory over sin every day, every hour, every moment. "Remember Jesus Christ risen from the dead" (II Timothy 2:8 R.V.).

R. A. TORREY

ONE LOOK FROM THEE

PROVERBS 28:13 ESV
Whoever conceals his transgressions will not prosper,
but he who confesses and forsakes them
will obtain mercy.

When darkness long has veil'd my mind,
    And smiling day once more appears;
Then, my Redeemer, then I find
The folly of my doubts and fears.

Oh! let me then at length be taught
What I am still so slow to learn,
That God is love, and changes not,
Nor knows the shadow of a turn.

Sweet truth, and easy to repeat!
But when my faith is sharply try'd,
I find myself a learner yet,
Unskilful, weak, and apt to slide.

But, O my Lord, one look from thee
Subdues the disobedient will;
Drives doubt and discontent away,
And thy rebellious worm is still.

WILLIAM COWPER

IT IS ENOUGH

HEBREWS 7:25 NLT
*Therefore he is able, once and forever, to save
everyone who comes to God through him.
He lives forever to plead with God on their behalf.*

O h, brethren, could you and I pass this day through
the heavens, and see what is now going on in the
sanctuary above— . . . could you see the Lamb with the
scars of his deep wounds in the very midst of the throne,
surrounded by all the odors—could you see the many
angels round about the throne, . . . and were one of these
angels to tell you, "This is He that undertook the cause of
lost sinners; He undertook to be the second Adam—the
man in their stead; and lo! there He is upon the throne of
heaven—consider Him. . . . Do you think His sufferings
and obedience will have been enough?—Yes, yes, every
soul exclaims, Lord, it is enough! . . . Yes, though the sins
of all the world were on my one wicked head, still I could
not doubt that His work is complete, and that I am quite
safe when I believe in Him.

ROBERT MURRAY MCCHEYNE

WHY GOD FORGIVES

1 JOHN 1:8–9 ESV

If we say we have no sin, we deceive ourselves,
and the truth is not in us. If we confess our sins,
he is faithful and just to forgive us our sins
and to cleanse us from all unrighteousness.

Seekers and inquirers have often voiced this deep question of concern: "Why does God forgive? and how does God forgive sin?" . . .

God knows that sin is the dark shadow standing between Him and His highest creation, man. God is more willing to remove that shadow than we are to have it removed!

He wants to forgive us—and that desire is a part of God's character. In the sacrificial death of a lamb in the Old Testament, God was telling us that one day a perfect Lamb would come to actually take away sin.

That is how and why God forgives sin now. In John's words: "We have an advocate with the Father, Jesus Christ the righteous: And he is the propitiation for our sins" (1 John 2:1–2a).

A. W. TOZER

The Blood of Christ

1 John 1:7 KJV

*But if we walk in the light, as he is in the light,
we have fellowship one with another, and the blood
of Jesus Christ his Son cleanseth us from all sin.*

An old minister who had preached the Gospel for fifty years was dying. He called for the Bible and said, "Find me the First Epistle of John, the first chapter and the seventh verse;" and when they found it for him he put his trembling finger on it and said, "I die in the faith of that verse." What is it? "The blood of Jesus Christ his Son cleanseth us from all sin."

. . . My friends, when Christ ascended to heaven he left his blood behind; it was shed on Calvary, and there it has remained for us. . . .

Now the blood is on the mercy-seat; while it is there God says, "I cannot see your sins, I am looking at the blood." O press toward the mercy-seat while the blood is on it, and God will accept your poor sinful souls for the sake of the blood of his Son.

Dwight L. Moody

THE WAY TO GOD

EPHESIANS 1:7 ESV
In him we have redemption through his blood,
the forgiveness of our trespasses,
according to the riches of his grace.

Jesus, my all, to heaven is gone,
He Whom I fix my hopes upon;
His track I see, and I'll pursue
The narrow way, till Him I view.
The way the holy prophets went,
The road that leads from banishment,
The King's highway of holiness,
I'll go, for all His paths are peace.

Lo! Glad I come; and Thou, blest Lamb,
Shalt take me to Thee, as I am;
Nothing but sin have I to give;
Nothing but love shall I receive.
Then will I tell to sinners round,
What a dear Savior I have found;
I'll point to Thy redeeming blood,
And say, "Behold the way to God."

JOHN CENNICK

SINKHOLE

LUKE 7:48 NLT
Then Jesus said to the woman,
"Your sins are forgiven."

Sin is a sinkhole. And, like a sinkhole, the results of sin are just as catastrophic. It swallows up everything in its path. Because of sin lives are ruined, families are wrecked, children are abused, people are murdered, lies are said, alcohol is abused, men and women lead promiscuous lives.

We can't leave it at this. The good news of the Gospel is that Jesus is Savior. Jesus saves us from sin. And He does this so that we can live rather than die. "You are to give him the name Jesus, because he will save his people from their sins."

That's what salvation really is: to bring from death to life. Think of a child who suddenly dashes into the middle of the road. A big truck is coming but the child does not notice. Someone jumps and grabs the child and keeps him from being run over. That's an act of salvation—from death to life.

ADRIAN DIELEMAN

GOD'S LOVING-KINDNESS

JOEL 2:12 NIV
*"Even now," declares the LORD, "return to me
with all your heart, with fasting
and weeping and mourning."*

This is the loving-kindness of God: He never turns His face away from a sincere repentance. God accepts and welcomes anyone who has become wicked to the greatest extreme and chooses to return towards the path of holiness. He does everything to restore such people to their former position. But God shows an even greater mercy: for those who demonstrate incomplete repentance, He still won't pass by their small and insignificant turn. Instead, He even gives these people a great reward. This is evident from what Isaiah the prophet says concerning the Jews. He said, "On account of his sin I put him to pain for a little while, and smote him, and turned my face away from him, and he was pained, and walked sorrowfully, and then I healed him, and comforted him." And we can also cite that most ungodly king who sinned by the influence of his wife. However, when all he did was mourn, put on sackcloth, and condemn his sin, he received the mercy of God.

CHRYSOSTOM

HE FORGIVES ALL OUR SINS

PSALM 103:2–3 NLT
*Praise the LORD, I tell myself, and never
forget the good things he does for me.
He forgives all my sins and heals all my diseases.*

W hat shall I render unto the Lord," that while I
remember these things my soul isn't appalled at
them? I will love You, Lord, thank You, and confess my
sins to Your name. You have wiped out my wicked and
sinful acts. Because of Your grace and mercy, You have
melted away my sin as though it were ice. Whatever evils
I haven't committed, I attribute to Your grace. For what
wouldn't I have committed, by loving sin for sin's sake?
Yes, everything that I confess You have pardoned. . . .
When whoever You call obeys Your voice and despises
the things I confess, don't let them despise me. I am sick
but was healed by the same Physician that healed them or
rather made them better. Because of this let them love
You much more. Let them see that You have restored me
from such great sin. Let them see themselves as weak and
in need of help.

AUGUSTINE

CHRIST OUR RIGHTEOUSNESS

HEBREWS 13:8 NIV
Jesus Christ is the same yesterday
and today and forever.

I saw with the eyes of my soul Jesus Christ at God's right hand; there, I say, was my righteousness; so that wherever I was, or whatever I was doing, God could not say of me, he wants my righteousness, for that was just before him. I also saw, moreover, that it was not my good frame of heart that made my righteousness better, nor yet my bad frame that made my righteousness worse, for my righteousness was Jesus Christ himself, "the same yesterday, today, and for ever" (Hebrews 13:8 TLB).

Now did my chains fall off my legs indeed. I was loosed from my afflictions and irons; my temptations also fled away; so that from that time those dreadful scriptures of God left off to trouble me; now went I also home rejoicing for the grace and love of God.

JOHN BUNYAN

FULL REDEMPTION

ISAIAH 55:7 NLT
Let the people turn from their wicked deeds.
Let them banish from their minds the very thought
of doing wrong! Let them turn to the LORD that
he may have mercy on them. Yes, turn to our God,
for he will abundantly pardon.

We need to remember that God is a God who is able to redeem even the failures caused by our sin. The blood of Jesus Christ is sufficient not only to cover our sin but to redeem the lives of those who are affected by our sin. This is not ever to get us to diminish the seriousness of our sin. By the way, it is not wrong to grieve and to mourn over how your sin has affected others. If we don't mourn in that way at times, then perhaps we've never seen the seriousness of our sin.

Some of us have seen the seriousness and are having a hard time getting up from the weight of that sin because of how others have been impacted. But remember that the same God who is in the process of redeeming your life from destruction is also at work in the lives of your children, your grandchildren, your mate, others who've been affected.

NANCY DEMOSS

NEVER LOSE SIGHT

LUKE 10:18–20 ESV

*And he said to them, "I saw Satan fall like lightning
from heaven. Behold, I have given you authority to
tread on serpents and scorpions, and over all the power
of the enemy, and nothing shall hurt you. Nevertheless,
do not rejoice in this, that the spirits are subject to you,
but rejoice that your names are written in heaven."*

One of the simplest and yet one of the mightiest
secrets of abiding joy and victory is to never lose
sight of Jesus.

. . . Over and over again, Satan will make an attempt to
discourage us by bringing up our sins and failures and
thus try to convince us that we are not children of God,
or not saved. If he succeeds in getting us to keep looking
at and brooding over our sins, he will soon get us discouraged, and discouragement means failure. But if we
will keep looking at what God looks at, the death of Jesus
Christ in our place that completely atones for every sin
that we ever committed, we will never be discouraged
because of the greatest of our sins. We shall see that while
our sins are great, very great, indeed they have all been
atoned for. Every time Satan brings up one of our sins, we
shall see that Jesus Christ has redeemed us from its curse
by being made a curse in our place (Galatians 3:13).

R. A. TORREY

Do Not Reject Christ

Isaiah 1:18 esv

Come now, let us reason together, says the LORD:
though your sins are like scarlet, they shall be
as white as snow; though they are red like
crimson, they shall become like wool.

The merit of Christ's blood is infinite; though your sins were greater than all sins, yet there is virtue in his blood to expiate them; for, it cleanses from all sin. Though the sands be many and large, yet the sea can overflow them all: so, though your sins be numerous and great, the blood of Christ can cover them all. In a word, the question is not about the greatness of your sins, but your present duty: be your sin what it will, the Lord calls you to come to Christ and receive him: and your unbelief in your rejecting Christ is greater than all your other sins; for it is a refusal of the remedy, whereby you may be relieved of all your sin and guilt. Your other sins are but against the law; but this sin, in rejecting Christ, is against the law and the gospel both.

RALPH ERSKINE

BLESSED ARE THE FORGIVEN

ROMANS 4:7–8 NASB
*Blessed are those whose lawless deeds have
been forgiven, and whose sins have been covered.
Blessed is the man whose sin the Lord
will not TAKE INTO ACCOUNT.*

Be content with what God gives thee. If he gives thee heaven, will he deny thee earth? He that bestows upon thee the pardon of sin, would surely pour into thy bosom the gold of both the Indies, were it necessary for thee. But thou hast got a greater happiness; for it is not said, Blessed is he that wallows in wealth, honour, and a confluence of worldly prosperity, but, "Blessed is he whose sin is forgiven, and whose iniquity is covered." . . .

Delightful and pleasant mercy. "He delights in pardoning mercy, as a father delights in his children. He is therefore called the Father of mercy" (Micah 7:18), "He pardons iniquity, and retains not his anger forever, because he delights in mercy." . . . This is pure mercy, to change the tribunal of justice into a throne of grace, to bestow pardons where he might inflict punishments, and to put on the deportment of a father instead of that of a judge.

STEPHEN CHARNOCK

GOD'S GREAT MERCY

PSALM 136:26 NRSV
*O give thanks to the God of heaven,
for his steadfast love endures forever.*

Thou, Lord, art ready to forgive, and art plenteous in mercy' (Psalm 86:5). A 'multitude of tender mercies' (Psalm 51:1). What arithmetic can count all the bubblings up of mercy in the breast of God, and all the glances and all the dispersals of his pardoning grace towards his creatures? And he keeps this mercy by him, as in a treasury, to this purpose: 'Keeping mercy for thousands, forgiving iniquity' (Exodus 34:7), and is still as full as ever, as the sun, which hath influenced so many animals and vegetables, and expelled so much darkness and cold, is still as a strong man able to run the same race, and perform by its light and heat the same operations.

STEPHEN CHARNOCK

ABOUT
LIVING THE
CHRISTIAN LIFE

—

I can do all things through Christ
who strengthens me.

PHILIPPIANS 4:13 NKJV

ABOUT LIVING THE CHRISTIAN LIFE

Jesus' promises about living the Christian life have as much to do with what He wants to do *in* you as they have to do with what He wants to do *through* you. Being the fallen creatures that we are, we tend to want to choose one or the other. God insists on doing both. Our desire to specify usually covers a selfish purpose (consistent with our human condition). We may desire God to work primarily *in* us because that will make us feel special, set apart, loved, and just a bit better off than anyone else. At other times, we may desire God to work *through* us without altering the channel, because we have our own plans and purposes—"Lord, can't you work through me without doing anything to me?"

As we will see in the following selections, God insists on shaping His tools even as He is using them. Those who submit to God's purposes find the delight of real purpose for their lives.

DELIGHTING IN GOD'S WILL

LEVITICUS 25:18 NIV
*Follow my decrees and be careful to obey my laws,
and you will live safely in the land.*

We have to form habits to express what God's grace has done in us. It is not a question of being saved from hell, but of being saved in order to manifest the life of the Son of God in our mortal flesh, and it is the disagreeable things which make us exhibit whether or not we are manifesting His life. Do I manifest the essential sweetness of the Son of God, or the essential irritation of "myself" apart from Him? The only thing that will enable me to enjoy the disagreeable is the keen enthusiasm of letting the life of the Son of God manifest itself in me. No matter how disagreeable a thing may be, say "Lord, I am delighted to obey Thee in this matter," and instantly the Son of God will press to the front, and there be manifested in my human life that which glorifies Jesus.

OSWALD CHAMBERS

GOD'S POWER IN THE CHURCH

JOHN 15:5 NIV
"I am the vine; you are the branches.
If a man remains in me and I in him,
he will bear much fruit;
apart from me you can do nothing."

He said to His disciples: "Ye shall receive power when the Holy Spirit is come upon you." Not many days after this, in answer to united and continued prayer, the Holy Spirit did come upon them, and they were all filled. Praise God, He remains with us still. The power given is not a gift from the Holy Spirit. He Himself is the power. Today He is as truly available, and as mighty in power, as He was on the day of Pentecost. But since the days before Pentecost, has the whole church ever put aside every other work and waited upon God for ten days, that that power might be manifested? We have given too much attention to method, and to machinery, and to resources, and too little to the source of power.

HUDSON TAYLOR

SLAVERY TO MONEY

PROVERBS 3:9–10 NIV
Honor the LORD with your wealth,
with the firstfruits of all your crops;
then your barns will be filled to overflowing,
and your vats will brim over with new wine.

I heard an interview with Bill Gates, and the interviewer asked him if he knew how rich he was, if he could really get his mind around it. He said he couldn't. "The only way I can understand it," he said, "is that there is nothing I can't buy. If I want something, I can have it." He said that Microsoft saved him because he was really more interested in what he was doing than how much money he had. "Lots of rich people are not happy," he said.

Sometimes I am glad I don't have very much money. I think money might own me if I had too much of it. I think I would buy things and not be satisfied with the things I have so I would have to buy more.

Jesus said it is harder for a rich man to enter the kingdom of heaven than for a camel to go through the eye of a needle.

DONALD MILLER

EXPANDED BY LONGING

MATTHEW 6:19–21 NCV

*"Don't store treasures for yourselves here on earth
where moths and rust will destroy them and thieves
can break in and steal them. But store your treasures
in heaven where they cannot be destroyed by moths
or rust and where thieves cannot break in and steal
them. Your heart will be where your treasure is."*

Thomas à Kempis declared, "Wait a little while, O my
soul, wait for the divine promise, and thou shalt have
abundance of all good things in heaven." In this posture
we discover that, indeed, we are expanded by longing.
Something grows in us, a capacity if you will, for life and
love and God. I think of Romans 8:24–25: "That is why
waiting does not diminish us, any more than waiting
diminishes a pregnant mother. We are enlarged in the
waiting. We, of course, don't see what is enlarging us. But
the longer we wait, the larger we become, and the more
joyful our expectancy" (*The Message*). There is actually a
sweet pain in longing if we will let it draw our hearts
homeward.

JOHN ELDREDGE

OUR EXAMPLE

1 PETER 2:9 NASB
But you are . . . A PEOPLE FOR God's
OWN POSSESSION, that you may proclaim
the excellencies of Him who has called you
out of darkness into His marvelous light.

Christ understood that being a "disciple" was in innermost and deepest harmony with what he said about himself. Christ claimed to be the way and the truth and the life (John 14:6). For this reason, he could never be satisfied with adherents who accepted his teaching—especially with those who in their lives ignored it or let things take their usual course. His whole life on earth, from beginning to end, was destined solely to have followers and to make admirers impossible.

Christ came into the world with the purpose of saving, not instructing it. At the same time—as is implied in his saving work—he came to be *the pattern,* to leave footprints for the person who would join him, who would become a follower. This is why Christ was born and lived and died in lowliness. It is absolutely impossible for anyone to sneak away from the Pattern with excuse and evasion on the basis that It, after all, possessed earthly and worldly advantages that he did not have.

SØREN KIERKEGAARD

MAKE USE OF YOUR TIME

EPHESIANS 2:8–10 NIV

*For it is by grace you have been saved, through faith—
and this not from yourselves, it is the gift of God—not
by works, so that no one can boast. For we are God's
workmanship, created in Christ Jesus to do good works,
which God prepared in advance for us to do.*

We ought to make the best possible use of God-
given opportunities and should not waste our
precious time by neglect or carelessness. Many people say:
there is plenty of time to do this or that; don't worry. But
they do not realize that if they do not make good use of
this short time, the habit formed now will be so ingrained
that when more time is given to us, this habit will become
our second nature and we shall waste that time also.
"Whoever is faithful in a very little is faithful also in
much" (Luke 16:10).

SADHU SUNDAR SINGH

THE PROCESS OF GOD'S CALL

ACTS 1:8 ESV

*"But you will receive power when the Holy Spirit
has come upon you, and you will be my witnesses
in Jerusalem and in all Judea and Samaria,
and to the end of the earth."*

Before sending Isaiah forth as his prophet, God showed him his glory. Exposed to that radiance Isaiah could only cry out in dismay, "Woe is me!" Prior to seeing the Lord, his lips were already unclean and he had already been dwelling in the midst of a people of unclean lips; yet he was unaware of all this . . . until that light shone down on him and he saw his actual state and theirs.

How could he now become God's mouthpiece, since his own lips were so defiled? The one thing that made it possible was his response in the face of God's holiness—this cry of "Woe!" Given such self-knowledge, he was ready for the seraph to come from the altar and cleanse his lips. Let us, then, keep the sequence in view, for it is a good one: first the uncleanness, then God's light, followed by the cry of self-knowledge, then the touch of cleansing, and finally the commission to go and serve.

WATCHMAN NEE

SALT AND LIGHT

JOHN 14:21 NASB

*"He who has My commandments and keeps them
is the one who loves Me; and he who loves Me
will be loved by My Father, and I will love him
and will disclose Myself to him."*

The disciples of Jesus have a purpose. Once they have linked their lives with his, and once Jesus has quenched their thirst so that its overflow touches the lives of others, the agenda is clear—be salt and be a light. *The followers of Jesus are to let their good deeds be seen; they are to stem corruption by being pure, they are to bear a winsome testimony for God, and they are to reflect the glory of God.* In short, they are the "salt of the earth." We have grown accustomed to this phrase representing dependability, solidness, kindness, purity, and respectability. That is what Christians are to be.

JAMES R. BECK

THE CARE OF THE SHEPHERD

JOHN 10:11 NIV

"I am the good shepherd.
The good shepherd lays down his life for the sheep."

A friend of mine . . . told me of one day meeting a shepherd, who had a large flock of sheep. . . .

"How in the world can you tell these sheep apart? They look all alike to me."

"Don't you see that that sheep has lost a little bit of wool? . . ." And so he went on describing each sheep by his faults and imperfections.

Ah, my friends, I am afraid that is the way the Good Shepherd knows some of us most easily.

But let us trust to the care of this Shepherd. He will take care of his flock. We read in the Scriptures that a lion and a bear once came and took a lamb out of David's flock, and he rose up against them, plucked the lamb out of their paws, and slew both the lion and the bear. How much more shall Jesus, the Good Shepherd, rescue the lambs of his flock from the power of the world and the wicked one!

DWIGHT L. MOODY

SEEK FIRST THE KINGDOM

MATTHEW 6:31–33 ESV

"Therefore do not be anxious, saying, 'What shall we eat?' or 'What shall we drink?' or 'What shall we wear?' For the Gentiles seek after all these things, and your heavenly Father knows that you need them all. But seek first the kingdom of God and his righteousness, and all these things will be added to you."

We cannot say to God, "I sought your kingdom first; now give me all the riches you promised." If we are truly seeking God's kingdom and its righteousness, then we will be indifferent to material prosperity (see Philippians 4:12). Jesus is not promising selfish people a sure-fire plan for getting all they want from God. He is assuring those who submit themselves to God's rule that they will have all they need. The emphasis of this saying is on the "first." Jesus does not deny that we have physical needs, but he is making it a question of priorities. We can think of all kinds of things that might come first in our lives before the kingdom of God. We might say to ourselves, "First, I must do this; then I must do that." The kingdom citizen's first task, however, is to seek wholeheartedly the kingdom of heaven. If we are doing that, we cannot be consumed by the anxious accumulation of material things. Then we will also know true security and peace of mind.

DAVID S. DOCKERY AND DAVID E. GARLAND

STRENGTH IN WEAKNESS

2 CORINTHIANS 12:9 NLT

Each time he said, "My gracious favor is all you need.
My power works best in your weakness."
So now I am glad to boast about my weaknesses,
so that the power of Christ may work through me.

And so, let me say, the God of Paul still lives; you have the same God Paul had. Oh, put your trust in God. Look to Him and pray to Him, and He will give you strength. He will make you stand. God has power enough; God has grace enough. God has strength enough to keep you on the straight path, if only you will look to Him, if only you will pray to Him daily for strength.

Let me warn you to put not your strength in yourself. When you are strong—when you think you are strong — then you are weak; that is the very time you are the weakest. Paul says, "When I am weak, then am I strong" (2 Corinthians 12:10). Our strength doesn't lie in ourselves; it lies in our Redeemer. If my strength is in myself, I will be constantly tumbling, constantly falling down. Therefore, keep a fast hold on God, who alone is able to make you stand.

DWIGHT L. MOODY

INNER TRANSFORMATION

ROMANS 12:2 NIV

Do not conform any longer to the pattern of this world,
but be transformed by the renewing of your mind.
Then you will be able to test and approve what God's
will is—his good, pleasing and perfect will.

When Paul replaces the list—the works—of the
flesh, he does not replace it with the works of
the law, but the fruit of the Spirit (Galatians 5:19–23).
The Christian alternative to immoral behaviors is not a
new list of moral behaviors. It is the triumphant power
and transformation of the Holy Spirit through faith in
Jesus Christ—our Savior, our Lord, our Treasure. "[God]
has made us competent to be ministers of a new covenant, not of the letter but of the Spirit. For the letter
kills, but the Spirit gives life" (2 Corinthians 3:6). So
transformation is a profound, blood-bought, Spirit-
wrought change from the inside out.

. . . You are free in Christ, because when you do from
the inside what you *love* to do, you are free, if what you
love to do is what you *ought* to do. And that's what transformation means: when you are transformed in Christ
you *love* to do what you *ought* to do. That's freedom.

JOHN PIPER

FREEDOM IN TRUTH

JOHN 8:31–32 NIV
To the Jews who had believed him, Jesus said,
"If you hold to my teaching, you are really my disciples.
Then you will know the truth,
and the truth will set you free."

Truth and freedom are constant companions. Where you find one, you will always find the other. Freedom in any area of life comes from discovering the truth about it. And discovering truth in a particular area always results in freedom of some kind.

It is when a child accepts the truth that there is nothing to be afraid of that she is finally free from a fear of the dark. It is only when a little boy accepts the truth that his father can and will catch him that he finds the freedom to leave the security of the diving board and jump into the pool. Likewise, it is only as we accept the truth of all that Christ did for us at Calvary that we will begin to enjoy the freedom he provided.

CHARLES STANLEY

LIVING THE TRUTH

JOHN 8:31–32 NKJV

Then Jesus said to those Jews who believed Him,
"If you abide in My word, you are My disciples indeed.
And you shall know the truth,
and the truth shall make you free."

But how do I recognize that the subject matter of the Christian message is the truth? Here the Bible gives a strange answer: "Then Jesus said to the Jews who had believed in him, 'If you continue in my word, you are truly my disciples; and you will know the truth, and the truth will make you free'" (John 8:31–32). . . . Christ makes the promise: the one who dares to do, this is the one who will recognize the truth. Truth is recognized only in the course of living it.

And finally: the truth will make you free! This is the gift of truth. The person who is upheld and sustained by the power of truth is the freest of all—afraid of nothing, bound by nothing. No prejudgment, no weak backing off when faced by deceitful hopes, but bound to one thing, the One, the Truth that is the truth of God that confers validity on all other truth. Whoever abides in the truth of God is truly free.

DIETRICH BONHOEFFER

READY FOR EVERY GOOD WORK

LUKE 18:14 NLT

"I tell you, this sinner, not the Pharisee, returned home justified before God. For the proud will be humbled, but the humble will be honored."

Moreover, ye were all distinguished by humility, and were in no respect puffed up with pride, but yielded obedience rather than extorted it, and were more willing to give than to receive. Content with the provision which God had made for you and carefully attending to His words, ye were inwardly filled with His doctrine, and His sufferings were before your eyes. Thus a profound and abundant peace was given to you all, and ye had an insatiable desire for doing good, while a full outpouring of the Holy Spirit was upon you all. . . . Every kind of faction and schism was abominable in your sight. Ye mourned over the transgressions of your neighbors: their deficiencies you deemed your own. Ye never grudged any act of kindness, being "ready to every good work." Adorned by a thoroughly virtuous and religious life, ye did all things in the fear of God. The commandments and ordinances of the Lord were written upon the tablets of your hearts.

CLEMENT OF ROME

ASSURANCE OF SALVATION

MATTHEW 23:39 NRSV

"For I tell you, you will not see me again until you say, 'Blessed is the one who comes in the name of the Lord.'"

Hypocrites and other unregenerate men may deceive themselves with false hopes and carnal presumptions about their being in God's favor and about their being saved. Their presumptions will die with them. However, those who truly believe in the Lord Jesus, who honestly love Him and try to walk in good conscience before Him, may in this life be assured with certainty that they are in a state of grace. They may also rejoice in the hope of the glory of God, and they will never be ashamed of that hope.

This certainty is not based on the fallible hope of guesswork or probabilities. Rather, it is the infallible assurance of faith, established on the divine truth of the promises of salvation. There is also the inner evidence of spiritual insight, given to us by God, to which these promises are directed. And there is the testimony of the Spirit of adoption, witnessing with our spirits that we are the children of God.

WESTMINSTER CONFESSION OF FAITH

LAW AND GRACE

MATTHEW 11:28–30 NIV
"Come to me, all you who are weary and burdened,
and I will give you rest. Take my yoke upon you
and learn from me, for I am gentle and humble in heart,
and you will find rest for your souls. For my yoke
is easy and my burden is light."

From me there is great, patient endurance and kindness. Seeing such a weight of sins—murders and self-love and things more unnamable than these—I am long-suffering and bear with those who do these things, not despising them but waiting for them to repent. If ever they should repent and change their ways, I immediately forgive them, not remembering their former acts. But the law of Moses is not like this. When you sin, it immediately punishes the sinner. It knows no repentance. It promises no remission. When I make demands about the covenant, I am not so much preoccupied with investigating the things that happened. For me, it is enough that a soul choose what is good with a genuine resolution. But the law goes overboard, both adding more punishments to the smaller ones and cursing the transgressors. Therefore my yoke is good on account of forgiveness, and my burden is light because it is not a collection of customs and various observances but decisions of the soul.

THEODORE OF MOPSUESTIA

DOING GOD'S WILL

MATTHEW 5:6 ESV
*"Blessed are those who hunger and thirst for
righteousness, for they shall be satisfied."*

Reading Scripture is a personal encounter with God. God reveals himself to us through his Word by the Holy Spirit. Because this is an encounter with God, whatever you do next reveals what you believe about God, and it will determine whether you will truly experience God. You cannot experience God outside of doing his will. By following God, you will know and experience God's using your life.

When the disciples began to do what Jesus said, they saw how the multitudes were fed. When Moses obeyed God, the waters parted, and God's people were delivered from captivity. Throughout Scripture, men heard instructions from God and began to follow them; and in doing so, they experienced what God had said. Don't confuse understanding with doing. Some of us feel if we've read the Scripture and understand it that God's revelation is automatically going to happen. It won't automatically happen until we adjust our lives and begin to be obedient to what God has said.

HENRY BLACKABY AND TOM BLACKABY

USE YOUR GIFTS

1 CORINTHIANS 12:7 NLT
*A spiritual gift is given to each of us
as a means of helping the entire church.*

I began to see that the Holy Spirit never intended that
people who had gifts and abilities should bury them in
the earth, but rather, he commanded and stirred up such
people to the exercise of their gifts and sent out to work
those who were able and ready. And so, although I was
the most unworthy of all the saints, I set upon this work.

Though trembling, I used my gift to preach the blessed
gospel, in proportion to my faith, as God had showed me
in the holy Word of truth. When the word got around
that I was doing this, people came in by the hundreds
from all over to hear the Word preached. . . .

And when I saw that they were beginning to live dif-
ferently, and that their hearts were eagerly pressing after
the knowledge of Christ and rejoicing that God sent me
to them, then I began to conclude that God had blessed
his work through me. And so I rejoiced.

JOHN BUNYAN

LOVE ONE ANOTHER

PHILIPPIANS 2:12–13 NCV

*My dear friends, you have always obeyed God when
I was with you. It is even more important that you
obey now while I am away from you. Keep on working
to complete your salvation with fear and trembling,
because God is working in you to help you want
to do and be able to do what pleases him.*

If we are told to love all men as our neighbors—as
ourselves—then surely, when it comes to those with
whom we have the special bonds as fellow Christians—
having one Father through one Jesus Christ and being
indwelt by one Spirit—we can understand how over-
whelmingly important it is that all men be able to see an
observable love for those with whom we have these
special ties. Paul makes the double obligation clear in
Galatians 6:10: "As we have therefore opportunity, let us
do good unto all men, especially unto them who are of
the household of faith." He does not negate the command to do good to all men. But it is still not meaning-
less to add, "especially unto them who are of the
household of faith." This dual goal should be our Christian mentality, the set of our minds; we should be con-
sciously thinking about it and what it means in our
one-moment-at-a-time lives. It should be the attitude
that governs our outward observable actions.

FRANCIS A. SCHAEFFER

LOSING YOUR LIFE TO SAVE IT

MATTHEW 16:24–25 NASB

*Then Jesus said to His disciples, "If anyone wishes
to come after Me, let him deny himself, and take up
his cross, and follow Me. For whoever wishes
to save his life will lose it; but whoever
loses his life for My sake will find it."*

To save one's life" is not a negative expression in itself.
On the contrary, God wants us to save our own lives.
What Luke's Christ condemns is a saving of one's self in
which people try to realize their legitimate hopes through
their own actions, their own efforts, their own thoughts.
People miss what they are aiming to do, then, when they
try to save up their lives for themselves. God gives us a life
that belongs to us only when we give it to someone else.
This remarkable characteristic of human life can be
explained theologically because God is the foundation
and result of this life. The failure of self-justification can
be perceived even on the psychological level of interpersonal experience, because an existence that is purely concerned with oneself is a ruined existence, so long as it
lacks the quality and warmth of human communication.

FRANÇOIS BOVON

A NEW WAY OF THINKING

ROMANS 12:2 NCV

*Do not change yourselves to be like the people of
this world, but be changed within by a new way of
thinking. Then you will be able to decide what God
wants for you; you will know what is good
and pleasing to him and what is perfect.*

By this Paul shows that there is one form of this world
and another of the world to come. If there are those
who love this present life and the things which are in the
world, they are taken up with the form of the present age
and pay no attention to what is not seen. But the things
which are not seen are eternal, and they are being transformed and renewed in the form of the age to come. For
this reason the world does not acknowledge them but
hates them and persecutes them. But the angels of God,
who belong to the age to come, see that form. . . .

. . . Our mind is renewed by the practice of wisdom
and reflection on the Word of God and the spiritual
understanding of his law. The more one reads the Scriptures daily and the greater one's understanding is, the
more one is renewed always and every day.

ORIGEN

LOVE YOUR NEIGHBOR

GALATIANS 5:14 KJV

For all the law is fulfilled in one word, even in this;
Thou shalt love thy neighbour as thyself.

The model of Christ we are explicitly told to take as our example is that of Jesus, the suffering servant, who "when they hurled their insults at him, he did not retaliate; when he suffered, he made no threats. Instead, he entrusted himself to him who judges justly" (1 Peter 2:23). Only twice in Paul's letters did he speak explicitly of the believer's love for God (Romans 8:28; 2 Thessalonians 3:5 ESV), although much that he said presupposes Jesus' statement about the first and greatest of the commandments. But Paul's emphasis was on the Christian's love for his fellow human beings. At one point, he goes so far as to say, "The entire law is summed up in a single command: 'Love your neighbor as yourself'" (Galatians 5:14).

Why did Paul call the selfless love of neighbor the fulfilling of the whole law? Not because it is superior to the worship and adoration of God, but rather because it is the proof of it.

TIMOTHY GEORGE AND JOHN WOODBRIDGE

LISTENING

JAMES 1:19 NIV

My dear brothers, take note of this: Everyone should be quick to listen, slow to speak and slow to become angry.

Check out Christ with the woman at the well (John 4). He could have blown her away with an endless barrage of verbal artillery. He didn't. He genuinely listened when she spoke; He "listened slowly." He read the lines of anxiety on her face and felt the weight of guilt in her heart. As she talked, He peered deeply into the well of her soul. It wasn't long before she found herself completely open, yet not once did she feel forced or needlessly embarrassed. His secret? He listened. He studied every word, each expression. Even the tone of her voice.

What does it take? Several things. Rare qualities. Like caring. Time. Unselfishness. Concentration. Holding the other person in high esteem. Sensitivity. Tolerance. Patience. Self-control. And—perhaps most of all—allowing room for silence while the other person is thinking and trying to get the words out. Wise is the listener who doesn't feel compelled to fill up all the blank spaces with verbiage.

CHARLES SWINDOLL

FAITH AND LOVE

I JOHN 3:10 NKJV
*In this the children of God and the children
of the devil are manifest: Whoever does not practice
righteousness is not of God,
nor is he who does not love his brother.*

Luther, Calvin, and those who followed them insisted
that the fruit of justification is faith active in love. A
living faith expresses itself in works of love, in service to
the neighbor. Believers who have been made right with
God by faith no longer labor under the compulsion of the
law or the self centered need to serve others as a means
of enhancing their own status before God. The medieval
schema of salvation declared that it was necessary for faith
to be "formed by love" (*fides caritate formata*) to be effective for salvation. But Luther insisted that we are justified
by faith alone, not by faith mingled and fortified by the
loving deeds we have done for others. Thus while our
love for others does not make us righteous, when one has
been declared righteous by faith alone, godly love is the
result.

TIMOTHY GEORGE AND JOHN WOODBRIDGE

AUTHENTICITY

MATTHEW 5:20 NRSV

"For I tell you, unless your righteousness exceeds that of the scribes and Pharisees, you will never enter the kingdom of heaven."

The religion of Jesus is morality transfigured by spirituality; we have to be moral right down to the depths of our motives.

It cannot be too often emphasised that our Lord never asks us to do other than all that good upright men do, but He does ask that we do just those same things from an entirely different motive (see Matthew 5:20).

We should make less excuses for the weaknesses of a Christian than for any other man. A Christian has God's honour at stake.

When a man is regenerated and bears the Name of Christ, the Spirit of God will see to it that he is scrutinised by the world, and the more we are able to meet that scrutiny, the healthier will we be as Christians.

OSWALD CHAMBERS

LIVING BEFORE GOD

MATTHEW 6:2–4 NKJV

*"Therefore, when you do a charitable deed, do not
sound a trumpet before you as the hypocrites do in the
synagogues and in the streets, that they may have glory
from men. Assuredly, I say to you, they have their
reward. But when you do a charitable deed, do not let
your left hand know what your right hand is doing, that
your charitable deed may be in secret; and your Father
who sees in secret will Himself reward you openly."*

What we should seek when giving to the needy is
neither the praise of men, nor a ground for self-
commendation, but rather the approval of God. This is
implied in our Lord's reference to our right and left
hands. "By this expression," Calvin writes, "he means that
we ought to be satisfied with having God for our only
witness." Although we can keep our giving secret from
others, and to some extent secret even from ourselves, we
cannot keep it secret from God. No secrets are hidden
from him. *So your Father who sees in secret will reward you.*

To sum up, our Christian giving is to be . . . "before
God," who sees our secret heart and rewards us with the
discovery that, as Jesus said, "It is more blessed to give
to receive."

JOHN STOTT

FRIENDSHIP WITH JESUS

JOHN 15:14 NASB
"You are My friends if you do what I command you."

Jesus makes it clear that the members of the apostolic band are His friends (*cf.* Luke 12:4). But friendship depends on common aims and outlook, and thus Jesus qualifies "Ye are my friends" by "if ye do the things which I command you." Once again obedience is the test of discipleship. The friends of Jesus are those who habitually obey Him.

. . . The slave is no more than an instrument. It is not for him to enter intelligently into the purposes of his owner. His task is simply to do what he is told. But this is not the pattern of relationship between Jesus and His disciples. He has called them "friends." He has kept nothing back from them. He has revealed to them all that the Father has made known to Him.

LEON MORRIS

CHRIST'S YOKE

MATTHEW 11:29 ESV

"Take my yoke upon you, and learn from me,
for I am gentle and lowly in heart,
and you will find rest for your souls."

A fter the statement, "Learn of Me," Christ throws in the disconcerting qualification, *"Take My yoke upon you and learn of Me."* Why, if all this be true, does He call it *a yoke?* Why, while professing to give Rest, does He with the next breath whisper *"burden"?* Is the Christian life, after all, what its enemies take it for—an additional weight to the already great woe of life, some extra punctiliousness about duty, some painful devotion to observances, some heavy restriction and trammeling of all that is joyous and free in the world?

It is astounding how so glaring a misunderstanding of this plain sentence should ever have passed into currency. Did you ever stop to ask what a yoke is really for? Is it to be a burden to the animal which wears it? It is just the opposite. It is to make its burden light. A yoke is not an instrument of torture; it is an instrument of mercy.

HENRY DRUMMOND

THE TWO OPTIONS

JOHN 12:24 NKJV
"Most assuredly, I say to you, unless a grain of wheat falls into the ground and dies, it remains alone; but if it dies, it produces much grain."

As with the grain, so is it with each human life. One of two things you can do with your life; both you cannot do, and no third thing is possible. You may consume your life for your own present gratification and profit, to satisfy your present cravings and tastes and to secures the largest amount of immediate enjoyment to yourself—you may eat your life; or you may be content to put aside present enjoyment and profits of a selfish kind and devote your life to the uses of God and men.

. . . He that consumes his life now, spending it on himself . . . this man is losing his life; it comes to an end as certainly as the seed that is eaten. But he who devotes his life to other uses than his own gratification, this man, though he may often seem to lose his life, and often does lose it so far as present advantage goes, keeps it to life everlasting.

MARCUS DODS

POVERTY AND RICHES

MATTHEW 6:19–21 ESV

"Do not lay up for yourselves treasures on earth,
where moth and rust destroy and where thieves break in
and steal, but lay up for yourselves treasures in heaven,
where neither moth nor rust destroys and where thieves
do not break in and steal. For where your treasure is,
there your heart will be also."

Don't trust in riches, for such things are left here on earth. Only faith will accompany you. Righteousness will also go with you if faith has led the way. Why do riches entice you? "Ye were not redeemed with gold and silver," possessions, or silk garments, "from your vain conversation, but with the precious blood of Christ." So then, the rich are those who are heirs of God, joint heirs with Christ. . . . Don't reject a poor man. For when Christ was rich, He became poor. He became poor because of you so that, by His poverty, He could make you rich. So then, don't praise yourself as though you were rich. He sent out even His apostles without money and the first of them said: "Silver and gold have I none," but I have faith. I am rich enough in the name of Jesus, "which is above every name." . . . But if you want to be rich, you must be poor.

AMBROSE

GOD'S LIGHT

PHILIPPIANS 2:12–13 NIV

Therefore, my dear friends, as you have always obeyed—
not only in my presence, but now much more in my
absence—continue to work out your salvation with
fear and trembling, for it is God who works in you
to will and to act according to his good purpose.

God doesn't help us carry out sin, but without His help, we can't do what is right or fulfill every part of the law of righteousness. Just as light doesn't help us shut or avert our eyes, it helps us to see. In fact, the eye can't see at all unless the light helps it. In the same way, the light of our souls helps our mental sight through His light and we can do good through His righteousness. But if we turn away from Him, it is our own doing. We are then acting according to the wisdom of the flesh and have given in to our fleshly, lawless desires. Therefore, when we turn to God, He helps us; when we turn away from Him, He turns His back on us. Even then, He helps us turn to Him. Certainly, this isn't something the light does for the eyes. Therefore, when He commands, "Turn ye unto Me, and I will turn unto you," what else can we say but, "Help us follow Your commands"?

AUGUSTINE

IN TIMES
OF FEAR AND
WORRY

———

Do not fear, for I am with you;
do not anxiously look about you,
for I am your God.
ISAIAH 41:10 NASB

IN TIMES OF FEAR AND WORRY

When times of fear and worry invade your life, do they find it already occupied by God's promises? Or have you noticed that fear and worry regularly occupy your life and then you desperately seek an alliance with God and His promises in order to drive them out? Many of us alternate between these experiences. We enjoy God's promises for a season (as you are doing right now) and find fear and worry only hovering on the horizon. But if we set God's promises aside as artifacts we can display rather than weapons for our defense, we soon discover that fear and worry have infiltrated our lives again.

It's easier and wiser to keep fear and worry at bay than to expel them once they have invaded. We need to dwell on God's promises. This means that we not only need to think about them constantly, but also that we must live on them.

SAVIOR TO THE HELPLESS

1 JOHN 4:18 ESV
There is no fear in love, but perfect love casts out fear.
For fear has to do with punishment,
and whoever fears has not been perfected in love.

The infinite heart of the infinite God flows out in love toward our Lord Jesus Christ. And there is no fear in the bosom of Christ. All His fears are past. . . . You do not need to live another hour under your tormenting fears. Jesus Christ has borne the wrath of which you are afraid. He now stands refuge for the oppressed—a refuge in the time of trouble. Look to Christ, and your fear will be cast out. Come to the feet of Christ, and you will find rest. Call upon the name of the Lord, and you will be delivered.

You say you cannot look, nor come, nor cry, for you are helpless. Hear, then, and your soul shall live. Jesus is a Saviour to the helpless. Christ is not only a Saviour to those who are naked and empty, and have not goodness to recommend themselves, but He is a Saviour to those who are unable to give themselves to Him. You cannot be in too desperate a condition for Christ.

ROBERT MURRAY MCCHEYNE

HE CARES FOR YOU

1 PETER 5:7 NRSV
Cast all your anxiety on him,
because he cares for you.

Peter recognizes that a great barrier to putting others first and thinking of them as more important is the legitimate human concern "But who then will care for me?" The answer is that God himself will care for our needs. He is able to do so far better than we are (his hand is "mighty," v. 6), and he wants to do so, for he continually *cares* for his children. Therefore casting *all your anxieties* on him is the path to humility, freeing a person from constant concern for himself and enabling him or her truly to be concerned for the needs of others.

WAYNE GRUDEM

THE MEANING OF REST

MATTHEW 11:29 NIV
"Take my yoke upon you and learn from me,
for I am gentle and humble in heart,
and you will find rest for your souls."

It is only when we see what it was in Him that we can know what the word Rest means. It lies not in emotions, nor in the absence of emotions. It is the mind at leisure from itself. It is the perfect poise of the soul; the absolute adjustment of the inward man to the stress of all outward things; the repose of a heart set deep in God. . . .

Two painters each painted a picture to illustrate his conception of rest. The first chose for his scene a still, lone lake among the far-off mountains. The second threw on his canvas a thundering waterfall, with a fragile birch-tree bending over the foam; at the fork of a branch, almost wet with the cataract's spray, a robin sat on its nest. The first was only *Stagnation;* the last was Rest. For in Rest there are always two elements—tranquillity and energy; silence and turbulence; creation and destruction; fearlessness and fearfulness. This it was in Christ.

HENRY DRUMMOND

The Unknown Power of Christ

JOHN 11:21 NASB
*Martha then said to Jesus,
"Lord, if You had been here,
my brother would not have died."*

Of course she was wrong. The plain truth of the matter is that Lazarus had died just because, in a truer sense than Martha could understand, the Lord was there! She did not know that her brother's sickness was "not unto death," that is, it was not part of Death's campaign and triumph, but was directly ordered "for the glory of God." It was actually planned by the Love that permitted it to take its course, and was meant to set the stage for the mightiest display of Christ's power, the most convincing declaration of His Godhead. But this Martha could not know. She had to learn—and she did learn—that His love outstrips all fleetness of the human mind, that it is always ahead of the conceptions and prayers of His followers, that when the lesser is denied it is as a preparation for the gift of the greater, that the measure of His power is "exceeding abundantly above all that we ask or think"—be our thoughts never so extravagant.

J. STUART HOLDEN

OUR GUARDIAN

1 PETER 5:7 NLT
Give all your worries and cares to God,
for he cares about what happens to you.

May your angels, holy Son,
Guard our homes when day is done,
When at peace, our sleep is best:
Bid them watch us while we rest.

Prince of everything that is,
High Priest of the mysteries,
Let your angels, God supreme,
Tell us truth dressed as a dream.

May no terror and no fright
Spoil our slumber in the night;
Free from care our eyelids close;
Spirit, give us prompt repose.

We have laboured through the day:
Lift our burdens when we pray,
Then our souls in safety keep,
That our sleep be soft and deep.

COLUMBANUS

VALLEY OF VISION

2 THESSALONIANS 3:3 NIV
*But the Lord is faithful, and he will strengthen
and protect you from the evil one.*

Lord, high and holy, meek and lowly,
   Thou hast brought me to the valley of vision,
   where I live in the depths but see thee in the heights;
   hemmed in by mountains of sin I behold thy glory.

Let me learn by paradox
   that the way down is the way up,
   that to be low is to be high,
   that the broken heart is the healed heart,
   that the contrite spirit is the rejoicing spirit,
   that the repenting soul is the victorious soul,
   that to have nothing is to possess all,
   that to bear the cross is to wear the crown,
   that to give is to receive,
   that the valley is the place of vision.
Lord, in the daytime stars can be seen from deepest wells,
   and the deeper the wells the brighter thy stars shine;
Let me find thy light in my darkness,
               thy life in my death,
               thy joy in my sorrow, thy grace in my sin,
               thy riches in my poverty, thy glory in my
               valley.

UNKNOWN

OUR BURDEN BEARER

MATTHEW 11:30 ESV
*"For my yoke is easy,
and my burden is light."*

The Lord is our burden-bearer, and upon Him we must lay off every care. He says, in effect, "Be careful for nothing, but make your requests known to me, and I will attend to them all."

Be careful for *nothing*, He says, not even your service. Why? Because we are so utterly helpless that no matter how *careful* we were, our service would amount to nothing! What have we to do with thinking whether we are fit or not fit for service? The Master-workman surely has a right to use any tool He pleases for His own work, and it is plainly not the business of the tool to decide whether it is the right one to be used or not. He knows; and if He chooses to use us, of course we must be fit. And in truth, if we only knew it, our chief fitness is in our utter helplessness. His strength is made perfect, not in our strength, but in our weakness. Our strength is only a hindrance.

HANNAH WHITALL SMITH

THE PEACE OF CHRIST

*"I leave you peace; my peace I give you.
I do not give it to you as the world does.
So don't let your hearts be troubled or afraid."*

So, do not let your heart be troubled and do not be afraid. Believe in me and trust in my mercy. When you think yourself far from me, I am often closest to you. When you think that almost everything is lost, then often you are about to gain the greatest reward. All is not lost when things do not turn out the way you planned. . . .

I know your innermost thoughts, and I know that it is more helpful for your salvation that you should sometimes be left feeling flat and spiritually listless. If you always felt aglow with love and full of joy, you would soon become proud of your good fortune and pleased with yourself, thinking yourself to be something you are not. What I have given I can take away, and I can return it when I please. . . . I can quickly lift you up again and turn all your trouble into joy.

THOMAS À KEMPIS

OUR SHELTER

JOEL 3:16 NIV
*The LORD will roar from Zion and thunder
from Jerusalem; the earth and the sky will tremble.
But the LORD will be a refuge for his people,
a stronghold for the people of Israel.*

O God, our help in ages past,
Our hope for years to come,
Our shelter from the stormy blast,
And our eternal home.

Under the shadow of Thy throne
Thy saints have dwelt secure;
Sufficient is Thine arm alone,
And our defence is sure.

The busy tribes of flesh and blood,
With all their cares and fears,
Are carried downward by the flood,
And lost in following years.

O God, our help in ages past,
Our hope for years to come,
Be Thou our guard while troubles last.
And our eternal home.

ISSAC WATTS

WORSHIP IN THE HARD TIMES

HABAKKUK 3:18 KJV
Yet I will rejoice in the LORD,
I will joy in the God of my salvation.

Habakkuk was a prophet during a period of history when Israel was quite wicked. Habakkuk asked God to judge the wickedness of His people, and God obliged. But the prophet was astonished that God chose the Chaldeans to inflict this judgment. The Chaldeans (or Babylonians) were much more wicked than the Israelites. Habakkuk couldn't understand why God used a nation more deplorably evil to chasten His people. At the end of the brief book that bears his name, Habakkuk puts the intense conflict aside and worships his God in song. . . .

In a moment of deep discouragement, Habakkuk used music to lift himself up, even to the point where he said, "I am ready to jump for joy to the God of my salvation, and spin around because of who God is." David, too, used song to lift his spirit during the discouraging times of life. He was a great musician and poet—his Psalms are actually praise hymns to God.

DAVID JEREMIAH

PEACE WITH GOD

MICAH 7:8 ESV

Rejoice not over me, O my enemy; when I fall,
I shall rise; when I sit in darkness,
the LORD will be a light to me.

When trouble, restless fears, anxious fretfulness, strive to overpower the soul, our safety is in saying, "My God, I believe in Thy perfect goodness and wisdom and mercy. What Thou doest I cannot now understand; but I shall one day see it all plainly. Meanwhile I accept Thy will, whatever it may be, unquestioning, without reserve." There would be no restless disturbance, no sense of utter discomfort and discomposure in our souls, if we were quite free from any—it may be almost unconscious—opposition to God's will. But we do struggle against it, we do resist; and so long as that resistance endures we cannot be at peace. Peace, and even joy, are quite compatible with a great deal of pain—even mental pain—but never with a condition of antagonism or resistance.

H. L. SIDNEY LEAR

ENTRUSTING OUR WORK TO GOD

PSALM 22:10 NCV
*I have leaned on you since the day I was born;
you have been my God since my mother gave me birth.*

What is needed for happy effectual service is simply to put your work into the Lord's hand, and leave it there. Do not take it to Him in prayer, saying, "Lord, guide me, Lord, give me wisdom, Lord, arrange for me," and then arise from your knees, and take the burden all back, and try to guide and arrange for yourself. *Leave* it with the Lord, and remember that what you trust to Him you must not worry over nor feel anxious about. Trust and worry cannot go together.

HANNAH WHITALL SMITH

VICTORY FOR TODAY

LUKE 12:29-31 NLT

*"And don't worry about food—what to eat and drink.
Don't worry whether God will provide it for you.
These things dominate the thoughts of most people,
but your Father already knows your needs. He will
give you all you need from day to day if you make
the Kingdom of God your primary concern."*

The battle always has to be fought before the victory
is won, though many people think they must have
the victory *before* the battle. The conflict with worry and
fear is almost always there—each person must overcome
or be overcome. But we must fight each battle of our lives
in the strength of Jesus' victory. . . .

When we worry, we are carrying tomorrow's load with
today's strength, carrying two days in one. We are moving
into tomorrow ahead of time. There is just one day in the
calendar of action—today. The Holy Spirit does not give
a clear blueprint of our whole lives, but only of the
moments, one by one.

. . . We need to remember that we are children of God,
living within his constant care. God knows and is interested both in the hardest problems we face and the tiniest
details that concern us. He knows how to put everything
in place, like a jigsaw puzzle, to make a beautiful picture.

CORRIE TEN BOOM

A PLACE OF QUIET REST

PSALM 46:1 NIV
God is our refuge and strength,
an ever-present help in trouble.

There is a place of quiet rest
  Near to the heart of God,
A place where sin cannot molest,
Near to the heart of God.

O Jesus, blest Redeemer
Sent from the heart of God,
Hold us who wait before Thee
Near to the heart of God.

There is a place of comfort sweet
Near to the heart of God,
A place where we our Savior meet,
Near to the heart of God.

There is a place of full release
Near to the heart of God,
A place where all is joy and peace,
Near to the heart of God.

CLELAND BOYD MCAFEE

CHRIST BE WITH ME

DEUTERONOMY 31:8 NLT
"Do not be afraid or discouraged, for the LORD is the
one who goes before you. He will be with you;
he will neither fail you nor forsake you."

I bind unto myself today
The power of God to hold and lead,
His eye to watch, his might to stay,
His ear to hearken to my need.
The wisdom of my God to teach,
His hand to guide, his shield to ward;
The word of God to give me speech,
His heavenly host to be my guard.

Christ be with me, Christ within me,
Christ behind me, Christ before me,
Christ beside me, Christ to win me,
Christ to comfort and restore me,
Christ beneath me, Christ above me,
Christ in quiet, Christ in danger,
Christ in mouth of friend or stranger.

PATRICK OF IRELAND

AFFLICTIONS

JAMES 1:2–4 NIV

*Consider it pure joy, my brothers, whenever you
face trials of many kinds, because you know that
the testing of your faith develops perseverance.
Perseverance must finish its work so that you may
be mature and complete, not lacking anything.*

Afflictions are a powerful means to make us quicken
our pace in the way to our rest. They are God's rod
and spur. What a difference is there between our prayers
in health and in sickness; between our prosperity and our
adversity repentings! Even innocent Adam is likelier to
forget God in a paradise, than Joseph in a prison, or Job
upon a dung-hill. Solomon fell in the midst of pleasure
and prosperity, while wicked Manasseh was recovered in
his irons.

God seldom gives his people so sweet a foretaste of
their future rest, as in their deep afflictions. He keeps his
most precious cordials for the time of our greatest faint-
ings and dangers. Even the best saints seldom taste of the
delights of God, pure, spiritual, unmixed joys, in the time
of their prosperity, as they do in their deepest troubles.

RICHARD BAXTER

VICTORY OVER SATAN

LUKE 10:18–19 NIT

"Yes," he told them, "I saw Satan falling from heaven as a flash of lightning! And I have given you authority over all the power of the enemy."

Satan is an already conquered enemy. He has nothing, absolutely nothing to say against one who belongs to the Lord Jesus. By my unbelief or ignorance or letting go of my hold of the victory of Jesus, I may give Satan authority over me which otherwise he does not possess. But when I know by a living faith that I am one with the Lord Jesus and that the Lord lives in me, maintaining and carrying on in me that victory, Satan has no power over me. Victory "through the blood of the Lamb" is the strength of my life.

Only this faith can inspire courage and joy in the struggle. . . .

We need only to have our souls filled with the vision of Satan being cast out of heaven by Jesus to maintain the power and victory of His blood. We need only be filled with faith in the blood and that He Himself is with us. Then we also are "more than conquerors through Him who loved us" (Romans 8:37).

ANDREW MURRAY

WORRY

MATTHEW 6:34 ESV
*"Therefore do not be anxious about tomorrow,
for tomorrow will be anxious for itself.
Sufficient for the day is its own trouble."*

Worrying is stupid. The Bible says, "Do not worry about anything." If you are worrying, you are being disobedient. I had to understand that before I could stop doing it. First, I tried in my own strength—positive thinking, not fretting anymore. That approach was about as successful as attacking a lion with a toy pistol! Only the Lord can set you free through the Holy Spirit. . . .

If the Bible is true—and it is true!—fear, worrying, and anxiety actually question the trustworthiness of God. Then apparently we are saying, "God, you are not speaking the truth." In other words, "You are lying." Will we believe what the Lord tells us in Philippians 4:19—"My God will meet all your needs according to his glorious riches in Christ Jesus"—and in Hebrews 13:5—". . . never will I leave you; never will I forsake you"? These promises allow us to say with confidence, "The Lord is my helper, I will not fear; what can man do to me?"

CORRIE TEN BOOM

SIMPLE FAITH

"Let not your hearts be troubled.
Believe in God; believe also in me."

Martin Luther called this passage "the best and most comforting sermon that the Lord Christ delivered on earth, a treasure and a jewel not to be purchased with the world's goods." These verses become the foundation for comfort, not only for these disciples but also for us. If you ever get to the point in your life where you think you've run out of escapes and there aren't any more places where you can rest, you'll find a tremendously soft, downy pillow in John 14:1–6 . . .

If there is a single central message in Jesus' words, it is that the basis of comfort is simple, trusting faith. If you're discontent, worried, anxious, bewildered, perplexed, confused, agitated, or otherwise in need of comfort, the reason is that you don't trust Him like you should. If you really trust Christ, what do you have to worry about?

JOHN MACARTHUR

BOASTING IN WEAKNESS

2 CORINTHIANS 12:9 ESV

But he said to me, "My grace is sufficient for you,
for my power is made perfect in weakness." Therefore
I will boast all the more gladly of my weaknesses,
so that the power of Christ may rest upon me.

There is a famous poem about a monk who, in an old convent cell, painted pictures of martyrs and holy saints and the face of Christ with the crown of thorns. Some of his fellow monks called his pictures poor daubs.

One night, feeling the poverty of his work and longing to honor Christ with pictures as beautiful as those of other painters, he decided to cast his apparently inadequate paintings into the fire.

"He raised his eyes within his cell. Oh wonder!
There stood a visitor, thorn-crowned was He.
A sweet voice the silence rent asunder,
'I scorn no work that's done for love of me.'"

JOHN ALLAN LAVENDER

EVERYDAY RELIGION

EPHESIANS 6:13 NIV

Therefore put on the full armor of God, so that when the day of evil comes, you may be able to stand your ground, and after you have done everything, to stand.

Religion may be learned on Sunday, but it is lived in the week day's work. The torch of religion may be lit in the church, but it does its burning in the shop and on the street. Religion seeks its life in prayer, but it lives its life in deeds. It is planted in the closet, but it does its growing out in the world. It plumes itself for flight in songs of praise, but its actual flights are in works of love. It resolves and meditates on faithfulness as it reads its Christian lesson in the Book of Truth, but "faithful is that faithful does." It puts its armor on in all the aids and helps of the sanctuary as its dressing room, but it combats for the right, the noble, and the good in all the activities of practical existence, and its battle ground is the whole broad field of life.

JOHN DOUGHTY

ANSWERED PRAYER

JOHN 15:7 NLT
*"But if you stay joined to me and my words
remain in you, you may ask any request
you like, and it will be granted!"*

Your father wants to answer prayer. If you are abiding in Christ, and if his Word abides in you, then you will pray in his will and he will answer. "And this is the confidence which we have before Him, that if we ask anything according to His will, He hears us" (1 John 5:14). It has well been said that prayer is not getting man's will done in heaven, but getting God's will done on earth. It is not overcoming God's reluctance but laying hold of God's willingness.

What a joy it is to have God answer prayer! What confidence it gives you to know that you can take "everything to God in prayer" and he will hear and answer! He does not always give us what we ask, but he does give us what we need, *when we need it*. This is one of the evidences of abiding.

WARREN W. WIERSBE

Miracles

John 2:11 NKJV

*This beginning of signs Jesus did in Cana of Galilee,
and manifested His glory; and His disciples
believed in Him.*

The first miracle that Moses wrought was to turn the water into blood—that is, into death. Christ's first miracle was to turn water into wine—which means joy and life.

A great many are claiming that miracles can be accounted for by natural causes. Let me give you a little advice. If you go into a church and hear a minister make such a remark, take your hat and get out as quick as possible. . . . It is just bringing the Son of God down to the level of one of the mediums of the present day, and degrading the miracle to a sleight-of-hand performance. The idea that any one should be guilty of such a thing in regard to our Lord and Saviour! A miracle is a supernatural event and if a man will only admit one miracle, that settles the whole question: but the moment we doubt one we are doing just what the devil wants us to do—doubting God's word.

Dwight L. Moody

DO NOT LOSE HEART

2 CORINTHIANS 4:1 ESV
*Therefore, having this ministry by the mercy
of God, we do not lose heart.*

Nothing makes friends as well and holds them as firmly as affliction does. Nothing fastens and compacts the souls of believers as well. Nothing is as timely for us teachers so that the things we say will be heard. For when hearers are in an easy time, they become listless and lazy and seem to be annoyed with the speaker. But when they are in affliction and distress, they long deeply to listen. When a soul is distressed, it looks for comfort everywhere. . . . The afflicted soul doesn't want to be concerned about many things. It only wants peace and stillness. It is content to be done with the present things, even if nothing else follows. . . . Paul says, "Tribulation worketh patience, and patience experience, and experience hope, and hope maketh not ashamed" [Romans 5:3–5]. So then, don't sink in your afflictions, but give thanks in everything so that you may profit from them and please God.

CHRYSOSTOM

IN TIMES OF TRIAL

When you pass through the waters,
I will be with you; and through the rivers,
they shall not overwhelm you; when you
walk through fire you shall not be burned,
and the flame shall not consume you.

ISAIAH 43:2 ESV

IN TIMES OF TRIAL

God's promises do not make trials easy. Trials, by definition, are hard. We don't often accept this news happily. We would prefer that God's promises kept us from trials. Instead, we have Jesus' guarantee that trials await us—"In this world you will have trouble" (John 16:33b NIV). And the context of that promise doesn't give us any indication that God will remove the troubles. Jesus promises to provide peace before, during, and after the trial (John 16:33a), and cheer-causing hope during the trial when we remember that, "I have overcome the world" (John 16:33c).

God's promises provide relief and respite, not escape. Clothe yourself and arm yourself with them as you reflect on the following meditations. They will elevate your endurance.

THE GIFT OF REASON

1 THESSALONIANS 4:13 NASB

But we do not want you to be uninformed, brethren,
about those who are asleep, so that you will not
grieve as do the rest who have no hope.

B ring out the gift of reason God has stored in our
hearts. Then when troubles surround us, we will
remember that we are only human, and as we have
already seen and heard, that life is full of misfortunes. . . .
Above all, reason will tell us according to God's command
that we who trust Christ shouldn't grieve over those who
have died. For we hope in the Resurrection and in great
crowns of which the Master has stored to reward our
great patience. We must allow our wiser thoughts to
speak to us in this melody. Then perhaps we might experience slight relief from our troubles. I urge you to stand
firm, even if the blow is a heavy one. Don't fall under the
weight of your grief. Don't lose heart. Be perfectly
assured of this: although we can't understand why God
ordained such troubles, the One who is wise and who
loves us arranged them for us.

BASIL

COMFORT IN SUFFERING

MATTHEW 5:11–12 NCV
"People will insult you and hurt you. They will lie and say all kinds of evil things about you because you follow me. But when they do, you will be happy. Rejoice and be glad, because you have a great reward waiting for you in heaven."

The greatest comfort for those who suffer from false accusations is given by the words of Scripture. When sufferers are wounded by the lying words of an unbridled tongue, and feel the sharp stings of distress, they can remember the story of Joseph. For Joseph was an example of righteousness while suffering under a slanderous charge. . . . When they look at Joseph's model of purity, their pain is eased by the remedy the story provides. They find the same thing when they look at David, who Saul hunted like a tyrant. When David caught his enemy and let him go unharmed, he received comfort in his distress. Then there is the story of the Lord Christ Himself, Maker of the ages, Creator of all things, very God, and Son of the very God. Yet He was called a gluttonous man and a drunkard by the wicked Jews. Christ's suffering is not only comforting but provides great joy to those who suffer. For they are counted worthy of sharing the sufferings of the Lord.

THEODORET

THE REFINER'S FIRE

ZECHARIAH 13:9 NASB
*And I will bring the third part through the fire,
refine them as silver is refined, and test them as gold
is tested. They will call on My name, and I will
answer them; I will say, "They are My people,"
and they will say, "The LORD is my God."*

Refiners throw pieces of gold into the furnace to be tested and purified by the fire. In the same way, God allows human souls to be tested by troubles until they become pure, transparent, and have profited greatly from the process. Therefore, this is the greatest advantage we have. So then, we shouldn't be disturbed or discouraged when trials happen to us. For if refiners know how long to leave a piece of gold in the furnace, and when to draw it out, . . . how much better does God understand this process! When He sees that we have become purer, He frees us from our trials so that we won't be crushed and defeated by them. Therefore, we shouldn't retreat or lose heart when unexpected things happen to us. Instead, we should submit to the One who knows best and who will test our hearts by fire as long as He likes. He does this for a reason and for the good of those who are tried.

CHRYSOSTOM

GOD THE PERSON

ISAIAH 43:2 NIV

*When you pass through the waters, I will be with
you; and when you pass through the rivers,
they will not sweep over you. When you walk
through the fire, you will not be burned.*

Simply reading the Bible, I encountered not a misty
vapor but an actual Person. A Person as unique and
distinctive and colorful as any person I know. God has deep
emotions; he feels delight and frustration and anger. . . .

As I read through the Bible in my winter aerie, I marveled at how much God lets human beings affect him.
I was unprepared for the joy and anguish—in short, the
passion—of the God of the Universe. By studying
"about" God, by taming him and reducing him to words
and concepts that could be filed away in alphabetical
order, I had lost the force of the passionate relationship
God seeks above all else. The people who related to God
best—Abraham, Moses, David, Isaiah, Jeremiah—treated
him with startling familiarity. They talked to God as if he
were sitting in a chair beside them, as one might talk to a
counselor, a boss, a parent, or a lover. They treated him
like a person.

PHILIP YANCEY

THE PURPOSE OF TESTING

---

1 PETER 1:6–7 NASB

In this you greatly rejoice, even though now for a little while, if necessary, you have been distressed by various trials, so that the proof of your faith, being more precious than gold which is perishable, even though tested by fire, may be found to result in praise and glory and honor at the revelation of Jesus Christ.

What is God's purpose as He tests us? First, to test the strength of our faith that we might know where our strength is, or isn't. Secondly, to humble us, lest we think more confidently of our spiritual strength than we should. Thirdly, to wean us away from worldly things. Fourthly, to call us to a heavenly hope so that we live in the above and not in the below. Fifthly, to reveal what we really love. Sixthly, to teach us to value the blessing of God and to appreciate it as it comes to us out of the times of suffering. Seventh, to enable us to help others in their trial, to bear one another's burdens. And eighth, to develop enduring strength for greater usefulness so that God can thrust us into greater places of ministry and effectiveness.

JOHN MACARTHUR

LEARNING TO TRUST

1 PETER 1:6–7 NLT

*So be truly glad! There is wonderful joy ahead,
even though it is necessary for you
to endure many trials for a while.
These trials are only to test your faith, to show that it
is strong and pure. . . . So if your faith remains strong
after being tried by fiery trials, it will bring you much
praise and glory and honor on the day when
Jesus Christ is revealed to the whole world.*

This is the ultimate reason, from our standpoint, why God fills our lives with troubles and perplexities of one sort and another: it is *to ensure that we shall learn to hold him fast.* . . .

When we walk along a clear road feeling fine, and someone takes our arm to help us, as likely as not we shall impatiently shake him off; but when we are caught in rough country in the dark, with a storm getting up and our strength spent, and someone takes our arm to help us, we shall thankfully lean on him. And God wants us to feel that our way through life is rough and perplexing, so that we may learn thankfully to lean on him. Therefore he takes steps to drive us out of self-confidence to trust in himself—in the classical scriptural phrase for the secret of the godly life, to "wait on the Lord."

J. I. PACKER

MAKING THE MOST OF PAIN

ROMANS 8:28 NASB

And we know that God causes all things to
work together for good to those who love God,
to those who are called according to His purpose.

Pain, then, may prepare us for heaven, but such alchemy is far from automatic. To make effective use of pain as a means of laying up treasure in heaven calls for resolute and active participation on the part of the sufferer. Pain in itself is a sterile thing, but, like the plow that bites deep into the winter-bound earth releasing life-giving nutrients and allowing sun and air and rain to penetrate, pain can prepare the way for fruitfulness. The rest is up to us. We all know those, even Christians, who have let their pain and sorrow make them hard and bitter or querulous and critical. Pain may be God's messenger, but it is we who must see to it that we allow it to do God's work in our lives; and as we reach out to God for help in this endeavor, His grace will flood towards us like a river from a newly opened dam.

MARGARET CLARKSON

THE HEDGE OF SUFFERING

1 PETER 5:7 NLT
Give all your worries and cares to God,
for he cares about what happens to you.

For God does not ask His children to endure anything that He Himself has not first endured. In Jesus Christ the almighty God suffered Himself to be hedged about in a manner we shall never be able to comprehend, let alone be called upon to undergo.

. . . Unsullied Purity took upon Himself the abhorrent hedge of mortal sin, which encircled Him ever more closely until it did Him to death for our sakes. Our hedges are placed about us whether we will or not; His was entered into voluntarily for love of us, and from it He brought forth the richest fruit in the universe—eternal life. Cannot He who so willingly endured such unimaginable condescension for love of us be trusted to care for all that concerns us, even the hedges that seem so hard to understand?

If God has entrusted you with a hedge of suffering, let Him teach you how to live within it so that His holy purpose and His life-giving fruit may be fully accomplished through you!

MARGARET CLARKSON

BE STILL MY SOUL

PSALM 46:10 ESV
Be still, and know that I am God.

Be still, my soul: the Lord is on thy side;
    Bear patiently the cross of grief or pain;
Leave to thy God to order and provide;
In every change he faithful will remain.
Be still, my soul: thy best, thy heavenly Friend
Through thorny ways leads to a joyful end.

Be still, my soul: thy God doth undertake
To guide the future as he has the past.
Thy hope, thy confidence let nothing shake;
All now mysterious shall be bright at last.
Be still, my soul: the waves and winds still know
His voice who ruled them while he dwelt below.

Be still, my soul: the hour is hastening on
When we shall be forever with the Lord,
When disappointment, grief, and fear are gone,
Sorrow forgot, love's purest joys restored.
Be still, my soul: when change and tears are past,
All safe and blessed we shall meet at last.

KATHARINA VON SCHLEGEL

THE SCARS OF SIN

ISAIAH 43:2 ESV

*When you pass through the waters, I will be with you;
and through the rivers, they shall not overwhelm you;
when you walk through fire you shall not be burned,
and the flame shall not consume you.*

Quite probably others of you are living with scars brought on by past sins or failures. Although you have confessed and forsaken those ugly, bitter days, you can't seem to erase the backwash. Sometimes when you're alone the past slips up from behind like a freak ocean wave and overwhelms you. The scab is jarred loose. The wound stays inflamed and tender and you wonder if it will *ever* go away. Although it is unknown to others, you live in the fear of being found out and rejected.

Tucked away in a quiet corner of *every* life are wounds and scars. If they were not there, we would need no Physician. Nor would we need one another.

CHARLES SWINDOLL

LOOK PAST THE STORM

2 CORINTHIANS 4:17 NIV

*For our light and momentary troubles are achieving
for us an eternal glory that far outweighs them all.*

O that you could dwell in the knowledge and sense
of this: the Lord sees your sufferings with an eye of
pity and also is able to achieve some good through them.
He is able to bring life and wisdom to you through your
trials. He will one day give you dominion over that which
grieves and afflicts you.

Therefore, do not be grieved at your situation or be
discontented. Do not look at the difficulty of your condition, but instead, when the storm rages against you,
look up to him who can give you patience and can lift
your head over it all and cause you to grow. If the Lord
did not help us with his mighty arm, how often would
we fall! If God helps you in proportion to your problems,
you should have no reason to complain, but rather, to
bless his name.

ISAAC PENINGTON

STRANGERS IN THE WORLD

JAMES 1:2–3 NRSV
*My brothers and sisters, whenever you face trials
of any kind, consider it nothing but joy,
because you know that the testing
of your faith produces endurance.*

Sometimes it is good for us to have troubles and hardships, for they often call us back to our own hearts. Once there, we know ourselves to be strangers in this world, and we know that we may not believe in anything that it has to offer. Sometimes it is good that we put up with people speaking against us, and sometimes it is good that we be thought of as bad and flawed, even when we do good things and have good intentions. Such troubles are often aids to humility, and they protect us from pride. Indeed, we are sometimes better at seeking God when people have nothing but bad things to say about us and when they refuse to give us credit for the good things we have done! That being the case, we should so root ourselves in God that we do not need to look for comfort anywhere else.

THOMAS À KEMPIS

REJOICE AND BE GLAD

MATTHEW 5:10–12 KJV

Blessed are they which are persecuted for righteousness'
sake: for theirs is the kingdom of heaven. Blessed are ye,
when men shall revile you, and persecute you,
and shall say all manner of evil against you falsely,
for my sake. Rejoice, and be exceeding glad:
for great is your reward in heaven: for so persecuted
they the prophets which were before you.

How did Jesus expect his disciples to react under persecution? Verse 12: "Rejoice and be glad!" We are not to retaliate like an unbeliever, nor to sulk like a child, nor to lick our wounds in self-pity like a dog, nor just to grin and bear it like a Stoic, still less to pretend we enjoy it like a masochist. What then? We are to rejoice as a Christian should rejoice and even to "leap for joy." Why so? Partly because, Jesus added, "your reward is great in heaven" (12a). We may lose everything on earth, but we shall inherit everything in heaven . . . partly because persecution is a token of genuineness, a certificate of Christian authenticity, "for so men persecuted the prophets who were before you" (12b). If we are persecuted today, we belong to a noble succession. But the major reason why we should rejoice is because we are suffering, he said, "on my account" (11), on account of our loyalty to him.

JOHN STOTT

PATIENCE IN TRIALS

JAMES 1:2–4 NKJV

*My brethren, count it all joy when you fall into various
trials, knowing that the testing of your faith produces
patience. But let patience have its perfect work,
that you may be perfect and complete, lacking nothing.*

Patience is a willing acceptance of things that are bitter. The one who is patient does not complain about adversity but praises God at all times. Persecution, worries, and illness are willingly endured.

If sinners place burdens upon our backs, we will not be weighed down if we bear them patiently. They may bring us a little pain, but they also bring us a crown. Holy people welcome tribulations. They use them as guides to eternity.

You simply will not know if you are strong or weak unless you are tempted. If you are at peace, there is no way you can know whether or not you are patient. It is only when your attention is grasped by an injury that you will determine your degree of patience. . . .

The only way to protect yourself against the darts of an enemy is to smother the darts with the humility and the love of Christ.

RICHARD ROLLE

THE MEANING OF TRUST

HEBREWS 11:19 NLT

Abraham assumed that if Isaac died, God was able
to bring him back to life again. And in a sense,
Abraham did receive his son back from the dead.

It is one thing to rest in God's blessings, and another thing to rest in Himself; it is one thing to trust God when I have before my eyes the channel through which the blessing is to flow, and quite another thing to trust Him when that channel is entirely stopped up. This was what proved the excellency of Abraham's faith. He showed that he could not merely trust God for an innumerable seed while Isaac stood before him in health and vigor, but just as fully if he were a smoking victim on the altar. This was a high order of confidence in God—it was part by the Creator and in part by the creature. No; it rested on one solid pedestal, [namely], God Himself. "He accounted that God was able." He never accounted that Isaac was able. Isaac, without God, was nothing: God, without Isaac, was everything.

C. H. MACKINTOSH

LOOK TO CHRIST

PSALM 34:5 ESV
Those who look to him are radiant,
and their faces shall never be ashamed.

They looked unto him, and were lightened"; for when we look at God, as revealed in Jesus Christ our Lord, and behold the God-head as it is apparent in the incarnate Man who was born of the Virgin Mary and was crucified by Pontius Pilate, we do see that which enlightens the mind and casts rays of comfort into our awakened heart.

First, then, we shall look to the Lord Jesus Christ in His life. And here the troubled saint will find the most to enlighten. In the example, in the patience, in the sufferings of Jesus Christ, there are stars of glory to cheer the midnight darkness of the sky of your tribulation. Come hither, ye children of God, and whatever now are *your* distresses, whether they be temporal or spiritual, you shall find in the life of Jesus Christ and His sufferings, sufficient to cheer and comfort you if the Holy Spirit will now open your eyes to look unto Him.

C. H. SPURGEON

REMEMBER GOD'S WORD

PSALM 119:6 NLT
*Then I will not be disgraced
when I compare my life with your commands.*

Why is it that my thoughts so quickly wander away from God's word and that the word I need is often not there when I need it? Do I ever forget to eat or drink or sleep? Why then do I forget God's word? Because I am not yet able to say with the psalmist, "I will delight in your statutes." I do not forget that in which I delight. Whether or not I forget something is (not) a matter (of my intellect but) of the whole person, a matter of the heart. That on which I depend, body and soul, is something I cannot forget. . . .

Because God has spoken to us in history, and that means in the past, it is necessary to remember; a necessary daily exercise is to repeat what has been learned. Every day we must go back afresh to the saving acts of God in order to be able to go forward. This is why the Scripture warns us constantly and urgently not to forget.

DIETRICH BONHOEFFER

FREE TO PURSUE GOD

PSALM 112:7 NCV
*They won't be afraid of bad news;
their hearts are steady because
they trust the LORD.*

Our spirits cleave to the dust, in defiance to the dictates of our better judgments; and I believe the Lord seldom gives his people a considerable victory over this evil principle, until he has let them feel how deeply it is rooted in their hearts.

A considerable part of our trials are mercifully appointed to wean us from this propensity; and it is gradually weakened by the Lord's showing us at one time the vanity of the creature, and at another his own excellence and all-sufficiency, from hence arises a peaceful reliance upon the Lord; . . . when the hearts of others shake like the leaves of a tree, he is fixed, trusting in the Lord, who he believes *can* and *will* make good every loss, sweeten every bitter, and appoint all things to work together for his advantage. He sees that the time is short, lives upon the foretastes of glory, and therefore accounts not his life, or any inferior concernment, dear, so that he may finish his course with joy.

JOHN NEWTON

Like Us in All Things

Hebrews 2:10 NIV

*In bringing many sons to glory, it was fitting
that God, for whom and through whom
everything exists, should make the author
of their salvation perfect through suffering.*

Christ hath had experience of all trials whereinto any of his servants can fall: poverty, forsaking of friends, exile, imprisonment, hunger, nakedness, watching, weariness, pain of body, heaviness of heart, desertion as to sense, wrath and curse of God. Christ hath carried his feeling with him into heaven; he knew what poverty meaneth, what trouble of conscience, what heaviness of spirit meaneth. Christ could not so experimentally pity us, so feelingly pity us, if he were not like us in all things; his heart was entendered by experience, as a man that hath felt the gout and felt the stone. Israel knew the heart of a stranger; Christ knew the heart of a man that is left to the world's frowns and snares. He took a communion of our nature and miseries, as a pawn and pledge that he will pity us and help us.

Thomas Manton

THE HELP WE NEED

ROMANS 8:26 ESV
*Likewise the Spirit helps us in our weakness.
For we do not know what to pray for as we ought,
but the Spirit himself intercedes for us
with groanings too deep for words.*

Just as a sick man does not ask the doctor for things which will restore him to health but rather for things which his disease longs for, so likewise we, as long as we are languishing in the weakness of this life, will from time to time ask God for things which are not good for us. This is why the Spirit has to help us.

The weakness which the Spirit helps us with is our flesh. . . . Whenever the Holy Spirit sees our spirit struggling with the flesh and being drawn to it, he stretches out his hand and helps us in our weakness.

ORIGEN

THE SPIRIT'S HELP

ROMANS 8:26 NIV

In the same way, the Spirit helps us in our weakness.
We do not know what we ought to pray for,
but the Spirit himself intercedes for us
with groans that words cannot express.

It is clear from what follows that Paul is speaking here about the Holy Spirit . . . We do *not know how to pray us we ought* for two reasons. First, it is not yet clear what future we are hoping for or where we are heading, and second, many things in this life may seem positive but are in fact negative, and vice versa. Tribulation, for example, when it comes to a servant of God in order to test or correct him may seem futile to those who have less understanding. . . . But God often helps us through tribulation, and prosperity, which may be negative if it traps the soul with delight and the love of this life, is sought after in vain.

The Spirit sighs by making us sigh, arousing in us by his love a desire for the future life. The Lord your God tempts you so that he might know whether you love him, that is, to make you know, for nothing escapes God's notice.

AUGUSTINE

FINDING OUR LIFE IN GOD

2 PETER 1:4 NIV

*Through these he has given us his very great and
precious promises, so that through them you may
participate in the divine nature and escape the
corruption in the world caused by evil desires.*

What does it matter if external circumstances are
hard? Why should they not be! If we give way to
self-pity and indulge in the luxury of misery, we banish
God's riches from our own lives and hinder others from
entering into His provision. No sin is worse than the sin
of self-pity, because it obliterates God and puts self-
interest upon the throne. It opens our mouths to spit out
murmurings and our lives become craving spiritual
sponges; there is nothing lovely or generous about them.

When God is beginning to be satisfied with us He will
impoverish everything in the nature of fictitious wealth,
until we learn that all our fresh springs are in Him. If the
majesty and grace and power of God are not being manifested in us (not to our consciousness), God holds
us responsible. "God is able to make all grace abound"
[2 Corinthians 9:8], then learn to lavish the grace of God
on others. Be stamped with God's nature, and His blessing will come through you all the time.

OSWALD CHAMBERS

IN TIMES OF TEMPTATION

---

*No temptation has overtaken you that
is not common to man. God is faithful,
and he will not let you be tempted beyond
your ability, but with the temptation he
will also provide the way of escape,
that you may be able to endure it.*

1 CORINTHIANS 10:13 ESV

IN TIMES OF TEMPTATION

Jesus experienced temptation. When we are tempted, we are not visiting unfamiliar territory for Him. In fact, some of His best promises, as you are about to sample, declare what He will do for us in the midst of temptation.

Temptations are times of danger for us, but we can be equally armed and dangerous to temptation if we remember wonderful promises like these: "But remember that the temptations that come into your life are no different from what others experience. And God is faithful. He will keep the temptation from becoming so strong that you can't stand up against it. When you are tempted, he will show you a way out so that you will not give in to it" (1 Corinthians 10:13 NLT).

Allow God's word, reflected in the thoughts and experiences of other believers through the centuries, to equip you to take temptation in stride. Depend on God's strength until He shows you a way out.

FACING THE TEMPTER

*Because he himself was tested by what he suffered,
he is able to help those who are being tested.*

Our Lord's words to Peter, "But He turned and said
unto Peter, Get thee behind Me, Satan: thou art an
offence unto Me: for thou savourest not the things that be
of God, but those that be of men" (Matthew 16:23) crys-
tallise for us His authoritative view of the conclusions of
man's mind, when that mind has not been formed by the
Holy Spirit, [namely] that it is densely and satanically
incapable of understanding His form of thought.

Satan does not tempt to gross sins; the one thing he
tempts to is putting myself as master instead of God. . . .

How are we to face the tempter? By prayer? No. With
the Word of God? No. Face the tempter with Jesus
Christ, and He will apply the word of God to you, and
the temptation will cease. "For in that He Himself hath
suffered being tempted, He is able to succour them that
are tempted" (Hebrews 2:18).

OSWALD CHAMBERS

THE BENEFITS OF FEAR

1 JOHN 4:17 NLT
And as we live in God, our love grows more perfect.
So we will not be afraid on the day of judgment,
but we can face him with confidence because
we are like Christ here in this world.

If rulers don't terrify those who do good works, how will God, who is by nature good, terrify those who don't sin? Paul says, "If thou doest evil, be afraid," always using strict words with the churches after the Lord's example. Conscious of his own boldness and the hearers' weakness, he says to the Galatians, "Am I your enemy, because I tell you the truth?" Healthy people don't need doctors when they are strong, but those who are sick need a doctor's skill. In the same way, we who are sick from shameful lusts, excesses, and other flames of the passions need the Savior. And He administers not only mild but also stringent medicines. The bitter roots of fear then disintegrate the sores of our sins that eat us. Therefore, fear is beneficial if bitter. . . . All of humanity stands in need of Jesus so that we may not remain as obstinate sinners to the end and be condemned.

CLEMENT OF ALEXANDRIA

THE MARK OF A CHRISTIAN

MATTHEW 5:8 ESV
*"Blessed are the pure in heart,
for they shall see God."*

K nowing that he is about to leave, Jesus prepares his disciples for what is to come. It is here that he makes clear what will be the distinguishing mark of the Christian in John 13:33–35.

This passage reveals the mark that Jesus gives to label a Christian not just in one era or in one locality but at all times and all places until Jesus returns.

Notice that what he says here is not a description of a fact. It is a command which includes a condition: "A new command I give you: Love one another. As I have loved you, so you must love one another. By this all men will know that you are my disciples, *if* you love one another." An *if* is involved. If you obey, you will wear the badge Christ gave. . . .

The point is that it is possible to be a Christian without showing the mark, but if we expect non-Christians to know that we are Christians, we must show the mark.

FRANCIS A. SCHAEFFER

A WAY OF ESCAPE

1 CORINTHIANS 10:13 NIV

No temptation has seized you except what is common
to man. And God is faithful; he will not let you
be tempted beyond what you can bear.
But when you are tempted, he will also provide
a way out so that you can stand up under it.

No one is completely free of temptations because the source of temptation is in ourselves. We were born in sinful desire. When one temptation passes, another is on its way. We will always have temptation because we are sinners who lost our original innocence in the Garden. Many have tried to escape temptations only to find that they more grievously fall into them. We cannot win this battle by running away alone; the key to victory is true humility and patience; in them we overcome the enemy. . . .

We must not despair when we are tempted but, instead, seek God more fervently, asking for his help in this time of tribulation. Remember St. Paul's words of assurance, "God will make a way of escape from every temptation so that we may be able to bear it." Let us, therefore, humble ourselves before God and take shelter beneath his hand. God will lift up all who have a humble spirit and save them in all trials and tribulations.

THOMAS À KEMPIS

PURITY OF HEART

MATTHEW 5:8 NLT
*"God blesses those whose hearts are pure,
for they will see God."*

Purity of heart . . . is to will one thing, namely, full and total allegiance to God. So if we ask, Where in the gospels did Jesus explain purity of heart in this way, the answer would be Matthew 22:37, "You shall love the Lord your God with all your heart." Not with part of your heart. Not with a double or divided heart. That would be impurity. Purity of heart is no deception, no double-mindedness, no divided allegiance. . . . Purity of heart is to will one thing, namely, God's truth and God's value in everything we do. The aim of the pure heart is to align itself with the truth of God and magnify the worth of God. If you want to be pure in heart, pursue God with utter singlemindedness. Purity of heart is to will that one thing.

JOHN PIPER

MEMORIZING SCRIPTURE

PSALM 119:11 ESV
*I have stored up your word in my heart,
that I might not sin against you.*

The Bible refers to memorizing Scripture as storing up His Word in our hearts (Psalm 119:11). I love that picture. God wants us to tuck His promises into our hearts so that, no matter where we are or what we're doing, we can pull them out and be strengthened by their truth.

You might not think you're good at memorizing Scripture. That's okay. Don't give up. Work at it. God isn't keeping score. Even if it takes you longer than someone else, it's worth the effort.

And if you're already memorizing Scripture, practice what my friend Mike Bullmore calls "strategic scripture memory." Start with the gospel. All God's promises and commands are precious, but those verses that tell us of the Son of God who gave His life in our place are the most precious of all. Since you have to begin somewhere, why not start with the central message of the Bible?

C. J. MAHANEY

HE UNDERSTANDS OUR WEAKNESSES

HEBREWS 4:15–16 NLT

This High Priest of ours understands our weaknesses,
for he faced all of the same temptations we do,
yet he did not sin. So let us come boldly to the throne
of our gracious God. There we will receive his mercy,
and we will find grace to help us when we need it.

He isn't arbitrarily trying to spoil my fun; he lovingly wants to protect me from the emotional, physical, relational, and spiritual downside that can come when we indulge ourselves in temptations.

Actually, he's in my corner. "For we do not have a high priest who is unable to sympathize with our weaknesses," says the Bible, "but we have one who has been tempted in every way, just as we are—yet was without sin."

It's always easier to talk about dealing with temptation with someone who's been there. So now when I talk to Jesus about the pressures I'm under to compromise my morality or take ethical short-cuts, . . . I picture him saying, "I know, I know. Believe me, I understand. Here— let me help you."

And he does help. "God is faithful; he will not let you be tempted beyond what you can bear," the apostle Paul assured us. "But when you are tempted, he will also provide a way out so that you can stand up under it" [1 Corinthians 10:13].

LEE STROBEL

STRENGTH TO RESIST

MATTHEW 4:8–11 NRSV

Again, the devil took him to a very high mountain
and showed him all the kingdoms of the world and
their splendor; and he said to him, "All these
I will give you, if you will fall down and worship me."
Jesus said to him, "Away with you, Satan!
for it is written, 'Worship the Lord your God,
and serve only him.'" Then the devil left him,
and suddenly angels came and waited on him.

And here, my dear brethren, let me beseech you to go to Jesus Christ; tell him how you are assaulted by the evil one, who lies in wait for your souls; tell him you are not able to master him in your own strength; beg his assistance, and you shall find him ready to help you, ready to assist you, and to be your Guide, your Comforter, your Savior, your All; He will give you strength to resist the fiery darts of the devil; and, therefore, you can nowhere find one so proper to relieve you as Jesus Christ; he knows what it is to be tempted; he was tempted by Satan in the wilderness, and he will give you the assistance of his Spirit to resist the evil one, and then he will fly from you.

GEORGE WHITEFIELD

TRUE PURITY

MATTHEW 5:8 NIV
*"Blessed are the pure in heart,
for they will see God."*

The popular interpretation is to regard purity of heart as an expression for inward purity, for the quality of those who have been cleansed from moral—as opposed to ceremonial—defilement. And there is good biblical precedent for this, especially in the Psalms. It was recognized that no one could ascend the Lord's hill or stand in his holy place unless he had "clean hands and a pure heart. . . ."

This emphasis on the inward and moral, whether contrasted with the outward and ceremonial or the outward and physical, is certainly consistent with the whole Sermon on the Mount which requires heart-righteousness rather than mere rule-righteousness. Nevertheless, in the context of the other beatitudes, "purity of heart" seems to refer in some sense to our relationships. Professor Tasker defines the pure in heart as "the single-minded, who are free from the tyranny of a divided self." In this case the pure heart is the single heart and prepares the way for the "single eye" which Jesus mentions in the next chapter.

JOHN STOTT

THE GOSPEL'S DEMANDS

PHILIPPIANS 4:13 NASB
*I can do all things through Him
who strengthens me.*

Whether we struggle with the more obvious sins of drug or sexual addiction, or the subtle but equally evil sins of gossip or gluttony, the flesh is a persistent enemy. . . .

"Christianity is not difficult," an old friend observed. "It is impossible." We become especially convinced of this statement when we stare down the roaring throat of the gospel's demands. "If anyone comes to me and does not hate his father and mother, his wife and children, his brothers and sisters—yes, even his own life—he *cannot be my disciple.* . . . In the same way, any of you who does not give up everything he has *cannot be my disciple*" (Luke 14:26, 33, emphasis mine).

Jesus expects his disciples to commit and sacrifice all for his kingdom. But there is good news. Jesus knows we cannot meet these expectations in the power of human strength alone. Only the cross of Christ can empower us to overcome our selfish, fallen natures.

WILLIAM P. FARLEY

NOTHING IS IMPOSSIBLE

JOHN 15:5 ESV
"I am the vine; you are the branches.
Whoever abides in me and I in him,
he it is that bears much fruit,
for apart from me you can do nothing."

Apart from Him we can do nothing. Whilst we are abiding in Him nothing is impossible. The one purpose of our life should therefore be to remain in living and intense union with Christ, guarding against everything that would break it, employing every means of cementing and enlarging it. And just in proportion as we do so, we shall find His strength flowing into us for every possible emergency. We may not feel its presence, but we shall find it present whenever we begin to draw on it. There is no temptation which we cannot master; no privation which we cannot patiently bear; no difficulty with which we cannot cope; no work which we cannot perform; no confession or testimony which we cannot make, if only our souls are living in healthy union with Jesus Christ; for as our day or hour, so shall our strength be.

F. B. MEYER

THE OPPORTUNITY OF TEMPTATION

JAMES 1:2–3 NASB
Consider it all joy, my brethren,
when you encounter various trials,
knowing that the testing of your faith
produces endurance.

Temptation is surely an assault to be withstood, but at the same time it is an opportunity to be seized. Viewed in this light, life becomes inspiring, not in spite but because of its struggles, and we are able to greet the unseen with a cheer, counting it unmixed joy when we fall into the many temptations which, varied in form, dog our steps from the cradle to the grave. . . . The officer who is bidden by his general to a post of great responsibility, and so of hardship and peril, is thrilled with the joy of his task. An opportunity has been given him to prove himself worthy of great trust, which can be done only at the cost of great trouble.

This is a true picture of temptation. And the result of it all is a nature invigorated and refined, a character made capable of close friendship with God, to say nothing of the unmeasured joy that is the attendant of nobility of soul and stalwart Christian manhood.

CHARLES H. BRENT

THE ENDURANCE OF JESUS

HEBREWS 2:18 NIV
*Because he himself suffered when he was tempted,
he is able to help those who are being tempted.*

His transcendence, however, has made no difference to His humanity. Our author has already stated that, in order to "become a merciful and faithful and high priest," the Son of God had "in all things to be made like unto his brethren;" and that "he is able to succor them that are tempted" because "he himself hath suffered being tempted" (Hebrews 2:17–18). So here he repeats that Christians have in heaven a high priest with an unequalled capacity for sympathizing with them in all the dangers and sorrows and trials which come their way in life, because He Himself, by virtue of His likeness to them, was exposed to all these experiences. Yet He endured triumphantly every form of testing that man could endure. . . . Such endurance involves more, not less, than ordinary human suffering: sympathy with the sinner in his trial does not depend on the experience of sin but on the experience of the strength of the temptation to sin which only the sinless can know in its full intensity.

F. F. BRUCE

RESISTING THE DEVIL

JAMES 4:7–8 NASB

Submit therefore to God. Resist the devil and
he will flee from you. Draw near to God
and He will draw near to you.

While James has earlier stressed the person's own
evil tendency as being responsible for sin (1:14),
he recognizes here the role of a supra-personal evil being.
The word *diabolos* is used in the Septuagint to translate
stn, the Hebrew word which gives us the title "Satan."
The two titles are thus identical in meaning (cf. Revelation 20:2), both suggesting that one of the devil's primary
purposes is "to separate God and man." This separation
the Christian must *resist.* When he does, James promises
that the devil "will flee from you." Whatever power Satan
may have, the Christian can be absolutely certain that he
has been given the ability to overcome that power.

Instead of succumbing to Satan's desire to separate us
from God, we should "draw near" to him. God, James
promises, graciously responds by drawing near to us in
turn. . . . Those who sincerely repent and return to God
will find him, like the father of the prodigal son, eager to
receive back his erring children.

DOUGLAS J. MOO

HUMBLE YOURSELF

1 CORINTHIANS 10:13 KJV

*There hath no temptation taken you but such as is
common to man: but God is faithful, who will not suffer
you to be tempted above that ye are able; but will
with the temptation also make a way to escape,
that ye may be able to bear it.*

No one is so perfect and so holy that he does not
sometimes have temptations; we cannot be without
them entirely. Yet, temptations are often very good for a
person, granted that they are troublesome and unpleasant,
for through them one is humbled, cleansed, and in-
structed. All the saints have passed through many trials
and temptations and have profited from them. Those who
could not deal with temptations have become lost and
have fallen away. . . .

Some people suffer terrible temptations at the beginning of their lives with Christ. Some at the end. And some
suffer their entire lives. Some people are tempted lightly
enough, and this is according to God's wisdom and fair-
ness. God ponders the state and merits of all people, and
he arranges everything in advance for our well-being. . . .
So, let us humble our souls under God's hand in every
temptation and trouble, for he will save the humble in
spirit and raise them up.

THOMAS À KEMPIS

THE PURE IN HEART WILL SEE GOD

MATTHEW 5:8 NRSV

*"Blessed are the pure in heart,
for they will see God."*

God is the giver of the pure heart, and he gives it for this very end, that it may be prepared for the blessedness of seeing him. Thus we are taught in the Scriptures. The people of God are sanctified, and their hearts are made pure, that they may be prepared for glory, as vessels are prepared by the potter for the use he designs. . . .

The time is coming when they shall assuredly see him. They shall see him who is infinitely greater than all the kings of the earth. They shall see him face to face, shall see as much of his glory and beauty as the eyes of their souls are capable of beholding. They shall not only see him for a few moments, or an hour, but they shall dwell in his presence, and shall sit down forever to drink in the rays of his glory.

JONATHAN EDWARDS

ABOVE ALL THAT WE ASK

EPHESIANS 3:20 NKJV

*Now to Him who is able to do exceedingly
abundantly above all that we ask or think,
according to the power that works in us . . .*

He can do abundantly more than we *ask*. Oh! Says
the soul, that he would but do so much for me as I
could *ask* him to do! How happy a man should I then be.
But mark, the text doth not say, that God is able to do *all*
that we can *ask or think,* but that he is able to do *above* all,
yea, *abundantly* above all, yea, *exceeding* abundantly above
all that we ask or think. What a text is this! What a God
have we! God foresaw the sins of his people, and what
work the devil would make with their hearts about them,
and therefore to prevent their ruin by his temptation, he
has thus largely, as you see, expressed his love by his word.
Let us therefore, as has been bidden us, make this good
use of this doctrine of grace, as to cast ourselves upon this
love of God in the times of distress and temptation.

JOHN BUNYAN

TRUE PEACE OF MIND

GENESIS 4:7 ESV
*"If you do well, will you not be accepted?
And if you do not do well, sin is crouching
at the door. Its desire is for you,
but you must rule over it."*

When a man desires a thing too much, he at once becomes ill at ease. A proud and avaricious man never rests, whereas he who is poor and humble of heart lives in a world of peace. An unmortified man is quickly tempted and overcome in small, trifling evils; his spirit is weak, in a measure carnal and inclined to sensual things; he can hardly abstain from earthly desires. Hence it makes him sad to forego them; he is quick to anger if reproved. Yet if he satisfies his desires, remorse of conscience overwhelms him because he followed his passions and they did not lead to the peace he sought.

True peace of heart, then, is found in resisting passions, not in satisfying them. There is no peace in the carnal man, in the man given to vain attractions, but there is peace in the fervent and spiritual man.

THOMAS À KEMPIS

HOW TO OVERCOME THE WORLD

1 JOHN 5:4 NIV

For everyone born of God overcomes the world.
This is the victory that has overcome the world,
even our faith.

To John and to his generation, and to all men who have had the vision of God, the world is the blinding, seducing, terrifying reality. By the world John meant that merely earthly order and fashion and mode of life, with its hates, greeds, foul habits, and dark mutinies against goodness and truth.

The man who has had his moment of vision, who receives in every hour the energy of God's Holy Spirit, will face its temptations, endure its trials, and he will overcome. All the splendid achievements and all the victory over the wrong, and the tyranny, and the cruelty of the past, however strongly these have been entrenched, have been gained by men of faith. Nothing has been impossible to them. But only One has gotten Him the faultless victory. That One is Jesus, the beginner and the consummator of faith, who endured the Cross, and despised its shame, and is now set down in the victor's place at the right hand of God.

WILLIAM M. CLOW

OVERCOMING TEMPTATION

MARK 9:45, 47 ESV
"And if your foot causes you to sin, cut it off.
It is better for you to enter life lame than
with two feet to be thrown into hell.
And if your eye causes you to sin, tear it out.
It is better for you to enter the kingdom of God with
one eye than with two eyes to be thrown into hell."

The person who only runs away from temptation and does not tear it out by the root will not gain very much. In fact, for such a person, temptations will quickly return, and they will be even worse. If you patiently put up with them, you will gradually overcome your temptations better through God's grace than by your own harshness and self-assertion. When you are tempted, seek advice often, and never deal harshly with others who are tempted; instead, comfort them as you would have them comfort you.

THOMAS À KEMPIS

Eternal Possessions

Mark 8:35 NLT

*"If you try to keep your life for yourself, you will lose
it. But if you give up your life for my sake and for
the sake of the Good News, you will find true life."*

B ut woe to them who do not know the true state of
their own souls, and more woe to them who prize
this unhappy, flawed life as the highest good. Some people cling so tightly to life that, although they can scarcely
get the bare necessities by working or begging, they
would still be willing to live here forever, caring nothing
for the kingdom of God   And, indeed, in the end
these unfortunate people will know to their sorrow how
cheap and worthless were those things that were so
important to them. On the other hand, God's saints and
all the devout friends of Christ took no account of material possessions nor of what marked success in this life,
but their whole hope and intent focused on eternal possessions. All that they wished for was lifted up toward the
permanent and invisible, lest love of visible things should
drag them down to the lowest depths.

Thomas à Kempis

JOY OVERCOMES TEMPTATION

NEHEMIAH 8:10 NASB
"Do not be grieved, for the joy of the LORD is your strength."

T he man who possesses "the joy of the Lord," finds it his strength in another respect, that it fortifies him against temptation. What is there that he can be tempted with? He has more already than the world can offer him as a reward for treachery. He is already rich; who shall ensnare him with the wages of unrighteousness? He is already satisfied; who is he that can seduce him with pleasing baits? "Shall such a man as I flee?" . . . Such a man is, moreover, made strong to bear affliction; for all the sufferings put upon him are but a few drops of bitterness cast into his cup of bliss, to give a deeper tone to the sweetness which absorbs them.

C. H. SPURGEON

THE DISCIPLINE OF OBEDIENCE

HEBREWS 11:6 NIV
*And without faith it is impossible to please God,
because anyone who comes to him must believe
that he exists and that he rewards those
who earnestly seek him.*

I swear by myself, declares the Lord, that because you
have done this . . . I will surely bless you. . . ." (Genesis
22:15–19).

Abraham has reached the place where he is in touch
with the very nature of God. He understands now the
Reality of God. . . .

By the discipline of obedience, I get to the place where
Abraham was and I see Who God is. . . .

The promises of God are of no value to us until by
obedience we understand the nature of God.

We read some things in the Bible three hundred and
sixty-five times and they mean nothing to us, then all of
a sudden we see what God means, because in some particular we have obeyed God, and instantly His nature is
opened up. "All the promises of God in Him are yes, and
in Him Amen" [2 Corinthians 1:20].The "yes" must be
born of obedience; when by the obedience of our lives
we say "Amen" to a promise, then that promise is ours.

OSWALD CHAMBERS

OUR NEED FOR PRAYER

MATTHEW 7:7 ESV

Ask, and it will be given to you; seek, and you will find; knock, and it will be opened to you.

There is no better mirror in which to see your need than the Ten Commandments. In them you will find what you lack and what you should seek. You may find in them that you have a weak faith, small hope, and little love toward God. You may see that you do not praise and honor God as much as you praise and honor yourself. You may see that you do not love the Lord, your God, with all of your heart. When you see these things you should lay them before God, cry out to him and ask for help, and with all confidence expect help, believing that you are heard and that you will obtain mercy. . . . It is important when we have a need to go to God in prayer. I know, whenever I have prayed earnestly, that I have been heard and have obtained more than I prayed for. God sometimes delays, but He always comes.

MARTIN LUTHER

WHEN YOU
NEED
GUIDANCE

"I will never leave you nor forsake you."
HEBREWS 13:5 ESV

WHEN YOU NEED GUIDANCE

The previous section leads us directly to this one. We often find we need guidance when we have wandered into temptation or when we have just escaped. What to do now? Our desire for guidance is frequently challenged by our tendency toward impatience. We want God's direction—now!

One of the lessons of living boils down to this: the more we insist on God's immediate guidance, the more likely we are to reject it when it comes. If we develop the attitude that we can cajole or threaten God into revealing His plans according to our timetable, we will also find it easy to forget who has the final word. Guidance comes from many sources, most of them unreliable. God's guidance comes from an infallible source, and once we receive it, there are no other options. If we desire God above all else, we will discover that His guidance comes when we need it. Note how others have discovered this principle of waiting for God's promised guidance.

BE MY GUIDE

JEREMIAH 29:11–13 NIV
"For I know the plans I have for you,"
declares the Lord, "plans to prosper you and not
to harm you, plans to give you hope and a future.
Then you will call upon me and come and pray to me,
and I will listen to you. You will seek me and find
me when you seek me with all your heart."

Thy way, not mine, O Lord,
However dark it be!
Lead me by Thine own hand;
Choose out my path for me.
I dare not choose my lot:
I would not, if I might;
Choose Thou for me, my God,
So shall I walk aright.

Choose Thou for me my friends,
My sickness, or my health;
Choose Thou my cares for me,
My poverty or wealth.
Not mine, not mine the choice,
In things great or small;
Be Thou my Guide, my Strength,
My Wisdom, and my All.

HORATIUS BONAR

SET THE LORD BEFORE YOU

ISAIAH 30:21 NASB

Your ears will hear a word behind you,
"This is the way, walk in it," whenever
you turn to the right or to the left.

What does it mean to set the Lord always before you? It means that you choose to relate everything you encounter to your trust in God. What you choose to focus on becomes the dominant influence in your life. You may be a Christian, but if your focus is always on your problems, your problems will determine the direction of your life. If your focus is on people, then people will determine what you think and do. In biblical times, the right hand was the most distinguished position, reserved for one's chief adviser and supporter. When you choose to focus on Christ, you invite Him to take the most important position in your life as Counselor and Defender. . . .

What an incredible act of God's grace that Christ should stand beside you to guide you and counsel you and defend you! How could you ever become dismayed over your situation with Christ at your right hand? What confidence this should give you!

HENRY BLACKABY AND RICHARD BLACKABY

HE LEADETH ME

PSALM 32:8 ESV
*I will instruct you and teach you
in the way you should go;
I will counsel you with my eye upon you.*

He leadeth me.
In pastures green? No, not always.
Sometimes He who knoweth best
In kindness leadeth me in weary ways
Where heavy shadows be;
Out of the sunshine warm and soft and bright,
Out of the sunshine into the darkest night.
I oft would yield to sorrow and to fright
Only for this: I know He holds my hand.
So, whether led in green, or desert land
I trust, although I cannot understand. . . .

So whether on the hilltops, high and fair
I dwell, or in the sunless valleys, where
The shadows lie —what matter? He is there.
And more than this; where'er the pathway lead
He gives to me no helpless, broken reed,
But His Own hand, sufficient for my need.
So where He leads me I can safely go.
And in the blest hereafter I shall know
Why in His wisdom He hath led me so.

UNKNOWN

YIELDING TO GOD

PROVERBS 3:6 NKJV
*In all your ways acknowledge Him,
and He shall direct your paths.*

"H e shall direct your paths" (v. 6, NKJV) is the promise, but the fulfillment of that promise is predicated on our obedience to the Lord. We must trust Him with all our heart and obey Him in all our ways. That means total commitment to Him (Romans 12:1–2). The word translated "trust" in verse 5 means "to lie helpless, facedown." It pictures a servant waiting for the master's command in readiness to obey, or a defeated soldier yielding himself to the conquering general.

The danger, of course, is that we lean on our own understanding and thereby miss God's will. This warning doesn't suggest that God's children turn off their brains and ignore their intelligence and common sense. It simply cautions us not to depend on our own wisdom and experience or the wisdom and experience of others. . . . When we become "wise in [our] own eyes" (Proverbs 3:7), then we're heading for trouble.

WARREN W. WIERSBE

TRUE SPIRITUAL POWER

MATTHEW 28:18–19 NLT

*Jesus came and told his disciples, "I have been given
complete authority in heaven and on earth. Therefore,
go and make disciples of all the nations."*

L et us be confident, Christian brethren, that our power
does not lie in the manger at Bethlehem nor in the
relics of the Cross. True spiritual power resides in the victory of the mighty, resurrected Lord of glory, who could
pronounce after spoiling death: "All power is given me in
heaven and in earth." . . .

Christ's resurrection brought about a startling change
of direction for the believers. Sadness and fear and
mourning marked the direction of their religion before
they knew that Jesus was raised from the dead—their
direction was towards the grave. When they heard the
angelic witness, "He is risen, as He said," the direction
immediately shifted away from the tomb—"He is risen,
indeed!" If this is not the meaning of Easter, the Christian
church is involved only in a shallow one-day festival each
year.

Thankfully, the resurrection morning was only the
beginning of a great, vast outreach that has never ended—
and will not end until our Lord Jesus Christ comes back
again!

A. W. TOZER

PARALYZED BY WORRY

MATTHEW 6:34 NLT
*"So don't worry about tomorrow,
for tomorrow will bring its own worries.
Today's trouble is enough for today."*

Jesus said, "Therefore do not be anxious for tomorrow; for tomorrow will care for itself. Each day has enough trouble of its own" (Matthew 6:34). He was saying, "Don't worry about the future. Even though it will have its share of problems, they have a way of working themselves out at the time. Just deal with them as they come, for there's no way to solve them in advance." Providing for tomorrow is good, but worrying about tomorrow is sin because God is the God of tomorrow just like He is the God of today. Lamentations 3:23 tells us His mercies "are new every morning." He feeds us like He fed the Children of Israel—with just enough manna for the day.

Worrying paralyzes you, making you too upset to accomplish anything productive. It will seek to do that to you by taking you mentally into tomorrow until you find something to worry about. Refuse to go along for the ride. The Lord says you have enough to deal with today. Apply today's resources to today's needs or you will lose today's joy.

JOHN MACARTHUR

THE LORD UPHOLDS US

PSALM 37:23–24 NIV
*If the LORD delights in a man's way, he makes
his steps firm; though he stumble, he will not fall,
for the LORD upholds him with his hand.*

Still more comfort! Not only are you to have plenty of temporal possessions; but everything you do, your whole life and conduct, will succeed and prosper, because you trust God, surrender yourself and your cause to Him, and remain yielded to Him throughout your life. . . . But this is opposed by the fact that a God-pleasing way of life receives no support but only hindrance and rejection from the wicked. This is a vexation for human nature. Therefore one must find consolation in God's approval and support of our way of life, regardless of the hindrance and rejection of the wicked.

. . . Here "falling" means that the righteous man is sometimes defeated and the wicked triumph. So it was with David, who was pursued by Saul and by Absalom, and with Christ, who was crucified. Such "falling" does not last long. God does not let the righteous man lie in rejection but takes hold of his hand, lifts him up, and causes him to remain standing.

MARTIN LUTHER

THE RIGHT TIME IS NOW

ECCLESIASTES 11:4 KJV
He that observeth the wind shall not sow;
and he that regardeth the clouds shall not reap.

He that observeth the wind shall not sow, and he that regardeth the clouds shall not reap." And this trite maxim, a summary of the imperative law of all husbandry, is not just a bit of mere moralizing. It is a positively protective counsel. For a farmer who knows his business does not wait until an ideal day encourages his sowing. Of course he cannot afford to. The proper season is at hand; he sows his seed; and trusts the disintegrating and reintegrating forces of Nature to keep that which he commits to them against the coming autumn.

So, too, our supreme life-duty must be carried on just as wholeheartedly, with just the same faith and courage, when conditions seem unpromising as when prospects flatter. If we wait for ideally favourable weather for the sowing of the good seed, for the investment of our lives in the field of human need and Divine fidelity, we shall die waiting.

J. STUART HOLDEN

HE GOES AHEAD OF US

JOHN 10:4 NRSV
"When he has brought out all his own,
he goes ahead of them, and the sheep follow
him because they know his voice."

Whatever awaits us is encountered first by Him—
each difficulty and complication, each wild beast
or wilder robber, each yawning chasm or precipitous
path. Faith's eye can always discern His majestic presence in
front; and when that cannot be seen, it is dangerous to
move forward. Bind this comfort to your heart: that the
Saviour has tried for Himself all the experiences through
which He asks you to pass; and He would not ask you to
pass through them unless He was sure that they were not
too difficult for your feet, or too trying for your strength.
. . . The Woodsman hews a path for us through the track-
less forest. The broad-shouldered Brother pushes a way
for us through the crowd. And we have only to follow.

This is the Blessed Life—not anxious to see far in front,
not careful about the next step, not eager to choose the
path, not weighted with the heavy responsibilities of the
future: but quietly following behind the Shepherd, *one step*
at a time.

F. B. MEYER

STEPING OUT IN FAITH

ROMANS 12:2 NLT

*Don't copy the behavior and customs of this world,
but let God transform you into a new person by
changing the way you think. Then you will know
what God wants you to do, and you will know how
good and pleasing and perfect his will really is.*

B ut how may we know God's will? That is not always
easy. Yet the difficulty is not in Him. He does not
wish us to grope painfully in the dark. . . . There is a more
excellent way. Let the heart be quieted and stilled in the
presence of God; . . . Let the voice of the Son of God
hush into perfect rest the storms that sweep the lake of the
inner life and ruffle its calm surface. Let the whole being
be centered on God Himself. And then, remembering
that all who lack wisdom are to ask it of God, and that
Jesus Christ is already made unto us wisdom, let us quietly appropriate Him, in that capacity, by faith; and then
go forward. . . . It is an immense help in any difficulty to
say, "I take thee, Lord Jesus, as my wisdom," and to do the
next thing, nothing doubting, assured that He will not
permit those who trust in Him to be ashamed.

F. B. MEYER

God's Guidance

PSALM 25:9 ESV
*He leads the humble in what is right,
and teaches the humble his way.*

We recognize that it is only as God guides us that we can know what our duty is, which is another way of saying that, God guides His people by His Word, interpreted and applied by His Spirit. If therefore, we neglect the Bible, we cannot but remain in ignorance of the Divine will. The shrewdest calculation and the keenest foresight can never be adequate for our supreme need, nor be a substitute for the knowledge of the Divine mind. . . . The mere reading of the Scriptures will not give us guidance for the way; we must obediently seek therein, for our personal need, the will of God and this is done by *prayer*. If we ask, He will answer, but if His guidance of us is to be continuous, our asking must be the reflection of an *attitude* towards Him, on our part, of dependence and trust.

WILLIAM GRAHAM SCROGGIE

CONFIDENCE

1 JOHN 5:14 NKJV

Now this is the confidence that we have in Him, that if we ask anything according to His will, He hears us.

J ohn says: "This is the confidence we have in him." The word *confidence* is not sufficiently strong in the English, so the translators declare it is *boldness* that we have in Him. Others say: "This is the assurance that we have in Him." So, it takes the words *confidence, boldness* and *assurance* to express in our minds what John meant. . . .

This kind of teaching, that we can have confidence in God and He will give us that which we ask according to His will, is flatly rejected by the man of unbelief. He says it cannot be so, that he will not accept it, and he demands the proof of human reason. . . .

And yet, all of this time as the argument goes on, the man of faith is confident. The man of faith does not dare rest on human reason. He does not reject the place of human reason, but he knows there are things that human reason cannot do.

A. W. TOZER

WHEN YOU
NEED
STRENGTH

—

Now glory be to God! By his mighty power at work within us, he is able to accomplish infinitely more than we would ever dare to ask or hope.

EPHESIANS 3:20 NLT

WHEN YOU NEED STRENGTH

Here we find one of those surprising twists in spiritual reality. When we ask God for strength, He is most likely to offer us weakness. We hear this truth in Paul's anguished realization, "For when I am weak, then I am strong" (2 Corinthians 12:10 NIV). When we are painfully aware of our weaknesses, we have a choice. We can turn to God and ask Him to make us feel stronger in ourselves or turn to God and ask for help to depend more on His strength. We can ask for more of a limited resource, or we can trust in His unlimited resources. Sooner or later, we learn the lesson God wraps in powerlessness. God tells us, "My gracious favor is all you need. My power works best in your weakness" (2 Corinthians 12:9 NLT).

As you think with others about their adventures in finding strength, continually affirm your weakness, so that you might experience God's abundant strength.

THE HEROISM OF ENDURANCE

If you have raced with men on foot and they have worn you out, how can you compete with horses? If you stumble in safe country, how will you manage in the thickets by the Jordan?

Only a heroic soul could do the heroic work needed by Israel and by God, and it was the greatest heroism of all which was needed, the *heroism of endurance*.

Nothing worth doing can be done in this world without something of that iron resolution. It is the spirit which never knows defeat, which cannot be worn out, which has taken its stand and refuses to move. This is the "patience" about which the Bible is full, not the sickly counterfeit which so often passes for patience, but the power to bear, to suffer, to sacrifice, to endure all things, to die, harder still sometimes to continue to live. The whole world teaches that patience. Life in her struggle with nature is lavish of our resources. She is willing to sacrifice anything for the bare maintenance of existence meanwhile. Inch by inch each advance has to be gained, fought for, paid for, kept. It is the lesson of all history also, both for the individual and for a body of men who have espoused any cause.

HUGH BLACK

SUCCESS OUT OF FAILURE

JOHN 3:30 NRSV
"He must increase, but I must decrease."

Sometimes it looks as if God's servants fail. When Herod beheaded John the Baptist, it looked as if John's mission was a failure. But was it? The voice that rang through the valley of the Jordan rings through the whole world today. You can hear its echo upon the mountains and the valleys yet, "I must decrease, but He must increase." He held up Jesus Christ and introduced Him to the world, and Herod had not power to behead him until his life work had been accomplished. Stephen never preached but one sermon that we know of, and that was before the Sanhedrin; but how that sermon has been preached again and again all over the world! Out of his death probably came Paul, the greatest preacher the world has seen since Christ left this earth. If a man is sent by Jehovah, there is no such thing as failure.

DWIGHT L. MOODY

PRAYING IN SECRET

MATTHEW 6:6 NKJV
*But you, when you pray, go into your room,
and when you have shut your door, pray to
your Father who is in the secret place; and your
Father who sees in secret will reward you openly.*

When we pray, let our words and requests be disciplined, maintaining quietness and modesty. Let us consider ourselves as standing in God's sight. We must please the divine eyes both with the use of our body and with the tone of our voice. For, as it is characteristic for a shameless person to be noisy with his cries, it is fitting for the modest man to pray with calm requests. Moreover, the Lord told us to pray in secret, which is best suited to faith—in hidden and remote places and in our very bedrooms. Then we can know that God is present everywhere and hears and sees everything. In His abundant majesty, He enters even into hidden and secret places. It is written, "I am a God at hand, and not a God afar off. If a man shall hide himself in secret places, shall I not then see him? Do not I fill heaven and earth?" [Jeremiah 23:23–24]. And again: "The eyes of the Lord are in every place, beholding the evil and the good" [Proverbs 15:3].

CYPRIAN

JOY OUT OF MOURNING

MATTHEW 5:8 NLT
*"God blesses those whose hearts are pure,
for they will see God."*

How does Paul say, "Rejoice in the Lord always"? The joy he is speaking of springs from tears of mourning. For just as worldly joy comes with sorrow, godly tears produce never-ending, unfading joy. The harlot, who obtained more honor than virgins, experienced joy when seized by this fire. Thoroughly warmed by repentance, she was moved by her longing desire for Christ. She loosened her hair, drenched His holy feet with her tears, wiped them with her tresses, and poured out all the ointment. But these were only outward expressions. Those emotions in her mind were much more fervent—things only God could see. Therefore, everyone who hears of this woman rejoices with her, delights in her good works, and acquits her of every sin. If we, who are evil, judge her this way, imagine what sentence she obtained from God, who loves mankind.

CHRYSOSTOM

FACING OUR WEAKNESS

2 CORINTHIANS 12:9 NIV
*But he said to me, "My grace is sufficient for you,
for my power is made perfect in weakness." Therefore
I will boast all the more gladly about my weaknesses,
so that Christ's power may rest on me.*

So often in Scripture—from Moses to Paul—we see people humbly admitting their weakness first and then God filling them with his power. . . .

The longer we stubbornly resist the obvious—that we're ultimately powerless by ourselves—the deeper we sink into the mire. After all, we can't reach out and cling to God's strength if we're too busy straining to clutch our own self-sufficiency. . . .

Once we come face-to-face with the reality of our own weakness, we need to remind ourselves that we follow an all-powerful God who all throughout history has an uncanny track record of infusing his followers with strength. . . .

In other words, let yourself dwell on how he empowered Moses, strengthened David, undergirded Daniel, emboldened Peter, and supported Paul. Remember how time after time God has proven himself to be trustworthy.

LEE STROBEL

GIVE AWAY YOUR BURDENS

PSALM 55:22 NIV

Cast your cares on the LORD and he will sustain you;
he will never let the righteous fall.

A man was carrying a heavy load of grain down a
country road. . . . A man in a passing wagon noticed
his struggle, and, judging the sack to weigh at least fifty
pounds, he gently tugged on the reins and slowed his
horses. "Mister, you need a ride. Get up here with me,
and I'll take you."

Relieved, the tired man climbed up onto the seat and
settled in for the remainder of the trip to town. However,
he did not remove the loaded sack from his shoulder.

After a moment of silence, the compassionate driver
said with consternation, "Why don't you put that down
and relax?"

To his surprise, the first man replied, "Oh no! It's
enough to ask you to carry me without having you carry
this also."

. . . When you're tempted to carry your burdens by
yourself, stop and think about whom you are dealing
with. He is *God*—the Creator and Sustainer of the universe!

ADRIAN ROGERS

LONGING FOR GOD

PSALM 31:24 ESV
*Be strong, and let your heart take courage,
all you who wait for the LORD!*

We ask you, God of grace and eternal life, to increase and strengthen hope in us. Give us this virtue of the strong, this power of the confident, this courage of the unshakable. Make us always have a longing for you, the infinite plenitude of being. Make us always build on you and your fidelity, always hold fast without despondency to your might. Make us to be of this mind and produce this attitude in us by your Holy Spirit. Then, our Lord and God, we shall have the virtue of hope. Then we can courageously set about the task of our life again and again. Then we shall be animated by the joyful confidence that we are not working in vain. Then we shall do our work in the knowledge that in us and through us and, where our powers fail, without us, you the almighty, according to your good pleasure, are working to your honour and our salvation. Strengthen your hope in us.

KARL RAHNER

GOD IS ALWAYS PRESENT

PSALM 61:3 NLT
*For you are my safe refuge,
a fortress where my enemies cannot reach me.*

The Christian can have confidence under adverse circumstances, for God knows. Darkness and light are alike to Him. More than that, He knows both the way and the wayfarer. He knows me! He understands my sigh of heart, my searching for guidance. He knows the faith that declares, however falteringly and faintly, "Lord, I believe; help thou my unbelief!"

The Almighty does not abandon us in our moments of bewilderment. He is with us every moment although, like Job, we are not aware of His presence. We can be sure that "when he hath tried me, I shall come forth as gold;" sighing will become song; darkness will be changed to the delight of daybreak!

Thus there is always an "afterward" for us when we are disciplined by delay or distress. With assurance therefore we affirm with joy: ". . . he performeth the thing that is appointed for me" (Job 23: 12, 14).

V. RAYMOND EDMAN

LIVING FOR HEAVEN

HABAKKUK 3:19 NRSV
GOD, the Lord, is my strength;
he makes my feet like the feet of a deer,
and makes me tread upon the heights.

How were some of the saints so perfect and contemplative? They strove to subordinate all their earthly desires to heavenly ones, and by doing so they could cling to God from the very depths of their hearts and freely attend to him. We are too occupied with our own concerns and too interested in the passing affairs of the world. We seldom completely overcome a single fault, and we have little enthusiasm for our daily progress; thus, we remain cold and only vaguely interested in what we are doing. If we were not so absorbed in ourselves and if we were less confused in our own hearts, then we might savor divine things and experience something of heavenly contemplation. . . .

If we made an effort to stand firmly and courageously in the struggle, doubtless we should see the help of our Lord from heaven, for he is ready to help those who trust in his grace; he gives us occasions to fight that we may win.

THOMAS À KEMPIS

TRUSTING HIS PROMISE

EPHESIANS 3:20–21 NASB
*Now to Him who is able to do far more abundantly
beyond all that we ask or think, according
to the power that works within us, to Him be
the glory in the church and in Christ Jesus
to all generations forever and ever. Amen.*

Therefore the only thing necessary for us to do is to believe and to pray most confidently in Christ's name that God will give us strength, since he has erected his kingdom and this is his doing. It is he who without our help, counsel, thought, or effort has brought his kingdom forth and has advanced and preserved it to this day. I have no doubt that he will consummate it without our advice or assistance. Because "I know in whom I believe," as St. Paul says (II Timothy 1:12), I am certain that he will grant me more, do far more abundantly, and help and counsel us beyond all that we ask or think (Ephesians 3:20). He is called the Lord who can and will help in a wonderful, glorious, and mighty way, particularly when the need is the greatest. We are meant to be human beings, not divine. So let us take comfort in his word and, trusting his promise, call upon him confidently for deliverance in time of distress and he will help.

MARTIN LUTHER

COURAGE IN PRAYER

MATTHEW 11:30 NRSV
"For my yoke is easy, and my burden is light."

When entering the prayer chamber, we must come filled with faith and armed with courage. Nowhere else in the whole field of religious thought and activity is courage so necessary as in prayer. The successful prayer must be one without condition. We must believe that God is love and that, being love, He cannot harm us but must ever do us good. Then we must throw ourselves before Him and pray with boldness for whatever we know our good and His glory require, and the cost is no object! Whatever He in His love and wisdom would assess against us, we will accept with delight because it pleased Him. Prayers like that cannot go unanswered. The character and reputation of God guarantee their fulfillment.

We should always keep in mind the infinite loving kindness of God. No one need fear to put his life in His hands. His yoke is easy; His burden is light.

A. W. TOZER

HE RIDES ON THE STORMS

ISAIAH 41:10 NLT

*Don't be afraid, for I am with you. Do not be
dismayed, for I am your God. I will strengthen you.
I will help you. I will uphold you with
my victorious right hand.*

My brother, God never thwarts adverse circumstances; that is not His method. I have often been struck with these words—"He rideth upon the wings of the wind" [Psalm 18:10]. They are most suggestive. Our God does not *beat down* the storms that rise against Him; He rides upon them; He works through them. You are often surprised that so many thorny paths are allowed to be open for the good—how that aspiring boy Joseph is put in a dungeon—how that beautiful child Moses is cast into the Nile. You would have expected Providence to have interrupted the opening of these pits destined for destruction. Well, He might have done so; He might have said to the storm, "Peace, be still!" But there was a more excellent way—to ride upon it.

GEORGE MATHESON

I WILL UPHOLD YOU

ISAIAH 41:10 ESV
Fear not, for I am with you;
be not dismayed, for I am your God;
I will strengthen you, I will help you,
I will uphold you with my righteous right hand.

The words I spoke to God that midnight are still vivid in my memory. "I am here taking a stand for what I believe is right. But now I am afraid. The people are looking to me for leadership, and if I stand before them without strength and courage, they too will falter. I am at the end of my powers. I have nothing left. I've come to the point where I can't face it alone."

At that moment I experienced the presence of the Divine as I had never before experienced him. It seemed as though I could hear the quiet assurance of an inner voice, saying, "Stand up for righteousness, stand up for truth. God will be at your side forever." . . .

Three nights later, our home was bombed. Strangely enough, I accepted the word of the bombing calmly. My experience with God had given me a new strength and trust. I knew now that God is able to give us the interior resources to face the storms and problems of life.

MARTIN LUTHER KING, JR.

OUR RESTORER

PSALM 23:3 KJV
*He restoreth my soul: he leadeth me in the
paths of righteousness for his name's sake.*

THE third verse of the twenty-third psalm begins,
"He restoreth my soul." I love to think of Christ as
a Restorer. There are a good many of you who have
strayed away from the fold, who want to come back and
be restored to your first love; and this is just what the Lord
wants to do for you. If you are full of the joy of the
Lord, you will be full of power. Just pray today that the
Lord will now restore your soul; pray, as David did,
"Restore unto me the joy of thy salvation; and uphold me
with thy free spirit. Then will I teach transgressors thy
way; and sinners shall be converted unto thee" [Psalm
51:12–13]. . . .

It seems to me that every day I find Christians more
troubled about their coldness and distance from God. . . .
This psalm is for them; let them remember that the Lord
is able and willing to be a restorer unto them.

DWIGHT L. MOODY

ABOUT FAITH

I have been crucified with Christ; it is no longer I who live, but Christ lives in me; and the life which I now live in the flesh I live by faith in the Son of God, who loved me and gave Himself for me.

GALATIANS 2:20 NKJV

ABOUT FAITH

Although faith is often described in solitary terms, it is not a self-enclosed power or ability. It must have an object. Our faith is only as effective and real as the object in which our faith rests. God deeply appreciates a certain kind of faith. According to the writer of Hebrews, "So, you see, it is impossible to please God without faith. Anyone who wants to come to him must believe that there is a God and that he rewards those who sincerely seek him" (Hebrews 11:6 NLT). God rewards those who acknowledge His existence and seek Him.

Jesus illustrated repeatedly that the amount of faith required was quite small. What mattered was the identity of the One toward whom the faith was directed.

As you consider the following reflections on faith, stop wondering how big your faith is and focus instead on how amazing and magnificent God has revealed Himself to be.

I Can Do All Things

GALATIANS 3:3, 5 NLT

*Have you lost your senses? After starting your
Christian lives in the Spirit, why are you now
trying to become perfect by your own human effort? . . .
I ask you again, does God give you the Holy Spirit
and work miracles among you because you obey
the law of Moses? Of course not! It is because you
believe the message you heard about Christ.*

Think of the things you are trying to have faith for!
Stop thinking of them and think about your state in
God through receiving Christ Jesus; see how God has
enabled you to walk where you used to totter, and see
what marvellous strength you have in Him. "I can do all
things in Him that strengtheneth me" (Philippians 4:13
RV), says Paul. Is that mere poetry or a fact? Paul never
talked only poetry. All the great blessings of God in salvation and sanctification, all the Holy Spirit's illumination,
are ours not because we obey; they are ours because we
have put ourselves into a right relationship with God by
receiving Christ Jesus the Lord, and we obey spon-
taneously. As we look back we find that every time we
have been blessed it was not through mechanical obedience, but by receiving from Jesus something that
enabled us to obey without knowing it, and life was
flooded with the power of God.

OSWALD CHAMBERS

THE GOD WE WORSHIP

EPHESIANS 3:18–19 NRSV

*I pray that you may have the power to comprehend,
with all the saints, what is the breadth and
length and height and depth, and to know the love
of Christ that surpasses knowledge, so that you
may be filled with all the fullness of God.*

Our adoration of God should be done in faith, believing that He really lives in our hearts, and that He must be loved and served in spirit and in truth. Believe that He is the most independent One, upon Whom all of us depend, and that He is aware of everything that happens to us.

The Lord's perfections are truly beyond measure. By His infinite excellence and His sovereign place as both Creator and Savior, He has the right to possess us and all that exists in both heaven and earth. It should be His good pleasure to do with each of us whatever He chooses through all time and eternity. Because of all He is to us, we owe Him our thoughts, words, and actions. Let us earnestly endeavor to do this.

BROTHER LAWRENCE

GOD REVEALS HIMSELF

LUKE 10:22 NLT

*"My Father has given me authority over everything.
No one really knows the Son except the Father,
and no one really knows the Father except the Son
and those to whom the Son chooses to reveal him."*

He alone is capable of making Himself known as He
really is; we search in reasoning and in the sciences,
as in a poor copy, for what we neglect to see in an excellent
original. God Himself paints Himself in the depths of
our soul. We must enliven our faith and elevate ourselves
by means of that faith above all our feelings, to adore God
the Father and Jesus Christ in all Their divine perfections,
such as They are in Themselves. This way of faith is the
mind of the Church, and it suffices to arrive at high perfection.

BROTHER LAWRENCE

KEEP CLOSE TO GOD

JOHN 11:40 NIV
Then Jesus said, "Did I not tell you that if you believed, you would see the glory of God?"

I find that while faith is steady nothing can disquiet me, and when faith totters nothing can establish me. If I ramble out among means and creatures, I am presently lost, and can come to no end. But if I stay myself on God, and leave Him to work in His own way and time, I am at rest, and can lie down and sleep in a promise, though a thousand rise up against me. Therefore my way is not to cast beforehand, but to walk with God by the day. Keep close to God, and then you need fear nothing. Maintain secret and intimate acquaintance with Him, and then a little of the creature will go a great way. Crowd not religion into a corner of the day. Would men spend those hours they wear out in plots and devices in communion with God, and leave all on Him by venturesome believing, they would have more peace and comfort.

JOSEPH ELIOT

BEYOND APPEARANCES

MATTHEW 2:11 NASB
*After coming into the house they saw the
Child with Mary His mother; and they
fell to the ground and worshiped Him.*

Those who trust only their physical senses will not perceive the riches that hide beneath outward appearances. If you realize that the man in front of you is really your king in disguise as a commoner, you will treat him as a king. If you see the hand of God in ordinary events, even in disasters, you will accept whatever comes your way with respect and pleasure. You will welcome things that terrify others. They may be clothed in rags, but you will respect the majesty hidden beneath those rags.

Think of God's poverty as he lay crying and trembling on some hay in a manger! If you were to ask the citizens of Bethlehem their opinions of the baby Jesus, you would get ordinary responses. . . .

Now go ask Mary, Joseph, the shepherds, and the magi. They will tell you that in this absolute poverty they see something beyond words that is the glory of God. It is the very things which cannot be perceived by our senses that nourish and enlarge faith.

JEAN-PIERRE DE CAUSSADE

FAITH AND FRUIT

JAMES 2:17–18 NIV
*In the same way, faith by itself,
if it is not accompanied by action, is dead.
But someone will say, "You have faith; I have deeds."
Show me your faith without deeds, and I will
show you my faith by what I do.*

I want to speak to you this morning about work. Faith is the work of the mind, and work is the outward sign of faith. Some people talk about dead faith; but if faith is dead it ought to be buried, and so got out of the way. If it is dead it is not the faith of the Gospel, the faith which saves the soul. A true faith must work. . . .

In the fifteenth chapter of John, verses four and five, Christ says, "Abide in me, and I in you: . . . He that abideth in me, and I in him, the same bringeth forth much fruit." A good apple tree cannot help bringing forth apples; it does not have to try to do it. So it is with those who abide in Christ; they continually bring forth fruit. Now, abiding does not mean three or four weeks of special service, but three hundred and sixty-five days in a year of work for Christ.

DWIGHT L. MOODY

THE NATURE OF FAITH

ROMANS 10:9 NIV
*That if you confess with your mouth, "Jesus is Lord,"
and believe in your heart that God raised him
from the dead, you will be saved.*

There are three things that go to make up faith:
knowledge, assent, laying hold. A great many people
get as far as knowledge and the assent. They say, "O yes,
I believe; I assent," but they don't lay hold of the word of
God, and hold on to it for dear life. Faith is the basis of all
possible society. You just let men lose faith in one another,
and in the banks and business houses, and there would be
a terrible state of things. Well, the faith with which a man
believes in God is just the same kind of faith as that with
which he believes in his neighbor. The only difference is in
the object. Some people make a mistake right here. . . .
Faith is an outward look, and not an inward look. It looks
away from self to Christ; it looks over all mountains, and
up to God himself. It hears God speak, and it says,
"Amen! amen!"

DWIGHT L. MOODY

FAITH AND KNOWLEDGE

EPHESIANS 1:16–17 ESV

*I do not cease to give thanks for you, remembering you
in my prayers, that the God of our Lord Jesus Christ,
the Father of glory, may give you a spirit of wisdom
and of revelation in the knowledge of him.*

Contrary to the current secular understanding of
"faith," true New Testament faith is not something
that is made stronger by ignorance or by believing against
the evidence. Rather, saving faith is consistent with
knowledge and true understanding of facts. Paul says,
"Faith comes from hearing, and hearing by the word of
Christ" (Romans 10:17 NASB). When people have true
information about Christ, they are better able to put their
trust in him. Moreover, the more we know about him
and about the character of God that is completely
revealed in him, the more fully we are able to put our
trust in him. Thus faith is not weakened by knowledge
but should increase with more true knowledge.

In the case of saving faith in Christ, our knowledge of
him comes by believing a reliable testimony about him.
Here, the reliable testimony that we believe is the words
of Scripture. Since they are God's very words, they are
completely reliable, and we gain true knowledge of
Christ through them.

WAYNE GRUDEM

PRAYERLESSNESS

MATTHEW 6:6 NIV
*"But when you pray, go into your room, close the door
and pray to your Father, who is unseen.
Then your Father, who sees what is done
in secret, will reward you."*

At a subsequent meeting the opportunity was given for testimony as to what might be the sins which made the life of the church so feeble. Some began to mention failings that they had seen in other ministers, either in conduct, or in doctrine, or in service. It was soon felt that this was not the right way; each must acknowledge that in which he himself was guilty.

The Lord graciously so ordered it that we were gradually led to the sin of prayerlessness as one of the deepest roots of the evil. No one could plead himself free from this. Nothing so reveals the defective spiritual life in minister and congregation as the lack of believing and unceasing prayer. Prayer is in very deed the pulse of the spiritual life. It is the great means of bringing to minister and people the blessing and power of heaven. Persevering and believing prayer means a strong and an abundant life.

ANDREW MURRAY

PERSEVERANCE

HEBREWS 10:36 NASB
*For you have need of endurance,
so that when you have done the will of God,
you may receive what was promised.*

What we can see in the dark, the way we move when we cannot see where we are going, is different from what we can see in the light. When we have light, we can understand more and act accordingly. That can mean even taking risks or enduring hardships we could not see without the light. Doing the will of God requires that we not shrink from the contest of suffering. God does not promise that everyone will eventually come around to do the right thing, if we persevere. The Scripture does say that when we persevere, we do the will of God and will receive what he has promised.

HENRY BLACKABY AND TOM BLACKABY

FAITH AND HARDSHIP

ROMANS 8:28 NIV
*And we know that in all things God works
for the good of those who love him, who have
been called according to his purpose.*

In the middle of the loss of dear ones, or in the death of
a lifetime relationship, it is difficult to see the hand of
the God of life. Naomi, a refugee and a victim, found it
almost impossible to understand how her God could
bring something positive out of circumstances that
seemed to be the end of her world. In times like these, we
who suffer loss and marginalization in our own circumstances, need to stop to question our attitudes. Is it correct to blame God when we do not comprehend the
totality of human circumstances and relationships and
God's purposes in them? Significantly, the very poor in
Latin America seem never to lose their faith in God.
With perhaps exaggerated fatalism, they trust that God
who knows best will see them through, unaware of the
opportunities that God may provide to them to begin
changing their lives.

DALILA NAYAP-POT

THE ESSENCE OF FAITH

2 CORINTHIANS 4:6 ESV

For God, who said, "Let light shine out of darkness," has shone in our hearts to give the light of the knowledge of the glory of God in the face of Jesus Christ.

What then is the common essential element in all saving faith? What is it that makes believing in promises a saving act, rather than a deluded one like the experience of the hypocrites in Matthew 7:22? I have been putting it like this for some years: the essence of faith is "being satisfied with all that God is for us in Jesus." I think this is as close as I know how to get, because it gets at this idea of "delighting in" or "cherishing" or "consenting to" or "embracing" spiritual beauty.

Another way to say it would be that, in all the acts of saving faith, the Holy Spirit enables us not just to perceive and affirm factual truth, but also to apprehend and embrace spiritual beauty. . . . Spiritual beauty is the beauty of God diffused in all his works and words. Embracing this, or delighting in it, or being satisfied with it, is the heart of saving faith.

JOHN PIPER

THE FULLNESS OF DEITY

JOHN 20:27–29 NIV

Then he said to Thomas, "Put your finger here;
see my hands. Reach out your hand and put it
into my side. Stop doubting and believe."
Thomas said to him, "My Lord and my God!"
Then Jesus told him, "Because you have seen me,
you have believed; blessed are those who have
not seen and yet have believed."

It is, of course, a very big step intellectually (and emo-
tionally and morally as well, it will be found) to accept
this famous figure of history as the designed focusing of
God in human life. . . . Further, many people who have
a vague childish affection for a half-remembered Jesus,
have never used their adult critical faculties on the matter
at all. They hardly seem to see the paramount importance
of His claim to be God. Yet if for one moment we imagine the claim to be true, the mind almost reels at its significance. It can only mean that here is Truth, here is the
Character of God, the true Design for life, the authentic
Yardstick of values, the reliable confirming or correcting
of all gropings and inklings about Beauty, Truth, and
Goodness, about this world and the next. Life can never
be wholly dark or wholly futile if once the key to its
meaning is in our hands.

J. B. PHILLIPS

FAITH WITHOUT SIGHT

JOHN 20:27–29 NRSV

Then he said to Thomas, "Put your finger here and see my hands. Reach out your hand and put it in my side. Do not doubt but believe." Thomas answered him, "My Lord and my God!" Jesus said to him, "Have you believed because you have seen me? Blessed are those who have not seen and yet have come to believe."

Thomas believed on the basis of sight. He saw Jesus and believed. Some think that Jesus is administering a rebuke to His hard-headed follower. This may be, but if so, it is a very gentle rebuke. We must bear in mind that if it is true that Thomas believed only on the basis of what he himself saw, this is so also with all the others John has so far mentioned. . . . There is possibly significance also in the fact that when Jesus goes on to speak of those who believed without seeing He says "blessed," not "more blessed," are they. This does not look like a comparison, with Thomas worse off than the others. However, the Master does pronounce a blessing on those who have believed without seeing. . . . There is a special blessing for those possessed of a faith which can trust absolutely, and which does not need to "see" at every turn.

LEON MORRIS

Hold God's Faithfulness

MARK 11:22 NIV
"Have faith in God," Jesus answered.

Hold God's faithfulness. Abraham held God's faith and offered up Isaac, accounting that God was able to raise him up. Moses held God's faith and led the millions of Israel into the waste howling wilderness. Joshua knew Israel well and was ignorant neither of the fortifications of the Canaanites, nor of their martial prowess: but he held God's faithfulness and led Israel across Jordan. . . . All God's giants have been weak men who did great things for God because they reckoned on God being with them. . . .

Oh! beloved friends, if there is a living God, faithful and true, let us hold His faithfulness. Holding His faithfulness, we may go into every province of China. Holding His faithfulness, we may face, with calm and sober but confident assurance of victory, every difficulty and danger. We may count on grace for the work, on pecuniary aid, on needful facilities, and on ultimate success. Let us not give Him a partial trust, but daily, hourly, serve Him, "holding God's faithfulness."

HUDSON TAYLOR

DELIVERANCE FROM DOUBT

MATTHEW 28:17 KJV
*And when they saw him, they worshipped him:
but some doubted.*

Is doubt a sin? Not always. We should not, to begin with, say that doubt is the proper state for any mind; for if things were right, belief in the great spiritual realities would be as natural as seeing the light. Therefore doubt is unnatural, something that should not be, and from which we ought to seek escape. . . .

How shall we seek deliverance [from doubt]? By calm, reverential inquiry in the depths of the nature God has given us, and of that Word which professes to be the revelation of it and of Him—by humble, hopeful prayer to the Father of lights, whose will cannot be that any soul He has made should walk in darkness, . . . by an effort to be true ourselves and thoroughly genuine, . . . by a constant recurrence to the center and soul of things where we feel we can repose—the great assured character of God as a God of justice, love, and mercy, who will bring all right.

JOHN KER

BELIEVING GOD

ROMANS 4:20–21 NIV

Yet he did not waver through unbelief regarding the
promise of God, but was strengthened in his faith
and gave glory to God, being fully persuaded that
God had power to do what he had promised.

To believe that God is omnipotent, however strongly, with whatever full persuasion, when that belief is the mere admission of a dogma in theology, a general truth or proposition, proved by reason and affirmed in Scripture; so to believe and be fully persuaded and assured that what God has promised he is able also to perform; will go but a little way towards strengthening or establishing you in that faith which glorifies God. But let me again remind you that the faith in question is believing God, not believing something about God, but believing God. It is a personal dealing of God with you and of you with God. He and you come together; he to speak, you to hear; he to promise, you to believe; you to ask, he to give.

ROBERT S. CANDLISH

CHRIST THE ROCK

1 PETER 2:6–7 ESV

*For it stands in Scripture: "Behold, I am laying in
Zion a stone, a cornerstone chosen and precious,
and whoever believes in him will not be put to shame."
. . . But for those who do not believe, "The stone that
the builders rejected has become the cornerstone."*

There are many passages of Scripture where Christ is
portrayed as a rock or a stone. The prophet Daniel
calls him a stone which detaches itself without hands from
the mountain, hitting and threatening all the kingdoms
and filling the whole earth. This clearly refers to Christ.
And in the law the rock from which the waters flowed is
called Christ, as the apostle Paul himself testifies. And the
apostle Peter says to the Jews: this is the stone which the
builders rejected.

The Jews did not want to compare Christ's words with
his deeds lest perhaps they might recognize that it was not
absurd for him to say that he had come down from
heaven. . . . This was the rock of offense as far as the Jews
were concerned. The rock was undoubtedly the human
flesh of the Savior. It detached itself without hands,
because it was made of a virgin by the Holy Spirit without the participation of a male.

AMBROSIASTER

ABOUT
HIS PRESENCE
WITH YOU

"And surely I am with you always,
to the very end of the age."

MATTHEW 28:20 NIV

ABOUT HIS PRESENCE WITH YOU

Many of us can come up with a ready list of items we desire from God: answers, help, guidance, wisdom, and miscellaneous daily breads. What we seldom desire is God's presence. We might tolerate a divine guest in the background, but we shy away from asking God to be everywhere in our lives. We often want God available, but not present in such a way that He affects everything else. We tend to say, "God is always there for me," rather than "God is always here for me!"

God promises His presence anyway. It goes with His omnipresence! But we can ignore Him, and that often creates the illusion of His absence.

As you read the following reflections on God's promises regarding His indwelling presence, consider how life would be different if you made it a practice to acknowledge Him. Perhaps you will find some compelling reasons in the writings of other believers.

HAVE YOU MET GOD?

PHILIPPIANS 3:10 NIV
*I want to know Christ and the power
of his resurrection and the fellowship of sharing
in his sufferings, becoming like him
in his death.*

D o you know God? I am not asking whether you believe things about Him; but have you met Him? Have you known yourself for certain in His presence? Does He speak to you, and do you know that you speak to Him? . . . It matters not where you are as long as you know that this is possible, that Christ died to make it possible. He died "to bring us to God," and to this knowledge. . . . O that we might know God! Begin to cry with Job, "Oh, that I knew where I might find him," and you will soon find yourself desiring, hungering to know Him. The most vital question to ask about all who claim to be Christian is this: Have they a soul thirst for God? Do they long for this? Is there something about them that tells you that they are always waiting for His next manifestation of Himself? Is their life centred on Him? . . . "That I might know him!"

MARTYN LLOYD-JONES

DAY 274

HOW GOD TREATS HIS FRIENDS

PSALM 33:18 NLT
*But the LORD watches over those who fear him,
those who rely on his unfailing love.*

The secret of the Lord is with them that fear him. He deals familiarly with them. He calls them not servants only, but friends; and he treats them as friends. He affords them more than promises; for he . . . shows them . . . his favour towards them, the height, and depth, and length, and breadth of his love, which passeth knowledge. . . . And he permits and enables them to acquaint him with their cares, fears, wants, and troubles, with more freedom than they can unbosom themselves to their nearest earthly friends. His ear is always open to them; he is never weary of hearing their complaints and answering their petitions. The men of the world would account it a high honour and privilege to have an unrestrained liberty of access to an earthly king; but what words can express the privilege and honour of believers, who, whenever they please, have audience of the King of kings, whose compassion, mercy, and power, are, like his majesty, infinite.

JOHN NEWTON

FELLOWSHIP WITH GOD

PHILIPPIANS 3:10 NLT

As a result, I can really know Christ and experience the mighty power that raised him from the dead. I can learn what it means to suffer with him, sharing in his death.

Do not miss the blessedness of the fact that the fellowship of His sufferings means that He has fellowship with us. When I enter into the fellowship of His sufferings I am not alone, for He is forever with me. I can endure no pain for Him that He does not share with me. When I stand in the presence of sin and suffer—if I have climbed high enough, in that moment He is with me, He is feeling the same pain, He is suffering with me. When my heart is moved with hot anger because God is misunderstood, He is suffering with me. My fellowship with Him means His fellowship with me. When through pity born of His love my heart breaks over the awful punishment that is falling on the head of the sinner, never let Satan suggest I have reached a higher level than the Lord, for He is having fellowship with me; my pity is born of His pity, and His love is suffering with my love.

G. CAMPBELL MORGAN

LEAD ME

HEBREWS 13:5 NIV
"Never will I leave you; never will I forsake you."

I do not ask, O Lord, that life may be
　A pleasant road;
I do not ask that Thou wouldst take from me
　Aught of its load.

For one thing only, Lord, dear Lord, I plead:
　Lead me aright,
Though strength should falter and though heart should
　　bleed,
　Through peace to light.

I do not ask my cross to understand,
　My way to see;
Better in darkness just to feel Thy hand,
　And follow Thee.

Joy is like restless day; but peace divine
　Like quiet night.
Lead me, O Lord, till perfect day shall shine,
　Through peace to light.

A. A. PROCTER

THE CAVERNS OF TRUTH

JOHN 16:13 NIV

"But when he, the Spirit of truth, comes,
he will guide you into all truth.
He will not speak on his own;
he will speak only what he hears,
and he will tell you what is yet to come."

Truth may be compared to some cave or grotto. . . . Before entering the cavern you inquire for a guide, who comes with his lighted flambeau. He conducts you down to a considerable depth, and you find yourself in the midst of the cave. He leads you through different chambers. Here he points you to a little stream rushing from amid the rocks and indicates its rise and progress; there he points to some peculiar rock and tells you its name, then takes you into a large natural hall, tells you how many persons once feasted in it, and so on. Truth is a grand series of caverns; it is our glory to have so great and wise a conductor as the Holy Spirit. Imagine that we are coming to the darkness of it. He is a light shining in the midst of us to guide us. And by the light he shows us wondrous things. He teaches us by suggestion, direction, and illumination.

C. H. SPURGEON

THE PRESENCE OF GOD

ACTS 17:28 NIV
"For in him we live and move and have our being."
As some of your own poets have said,
"We are his offspring."

God is indeed there. He is there as He is here and everywhere, not confined to tree or stone, but free in the universe, near to everything, next to everyone, and through Jesus Christ immediately accessible to every loving heart. The doctrine of the divine omnipresence decides this forever.

This truth is to the convinced Christian a source of deep comfort in sorrow and of steadfast assurance in all the varied experiences of his life. To him "the practice of the presence of God" consists not of projecting an imaginary object from within his own mind and then seeking to realize its presence; it is rather to recognize the real presence of the One whom all sound theology declares to be already there, an objective entity, existing apart from any apprehension of Him on the part of His creatures.

A. W. TOZER

HE IS THERE

GALATIANS 2:20 NIV

*I have been crucified with Christ and I no longer live,
but Christ lives in me. The life I live in the body,
I live by faith in the Son of God, who loved me
and gave himself for me.*

We are surrounded by a generation that can find "no one home" in the universe. If anything marks our generation it is this. In contrast to this, as a Christian I know who I am; and I know the personal God who is there. I speak and He hears. I am not surrounded by mere mass, nor only energy particles, but He is there. And if I have accepted Christ as my Saviour, then though it will not be perfect in this life, yet moment by moment, on the basis of the finished work of Christ, this person-to-person relationship with the God who is there can have reality to me.

FRANCIS A. SCHAEFFER

CHRIST OUR REFUGE

PSALM 91:4 NIV
*He will cover you with his feathers,
and under his wings you will find refuge;
his faithfulness will be your shield and rampart.*

We live in an evil world, where we are liable to an abundance of sorrows and calamities. A great part of our lives is spent in sorrowing for present or past evils, and in fearing those which are future. What poor, distressed creatures are we. . . . If any person is taken sick and trembles for his life, or if our near friends are at the point of death or in many other dangers, how fearful is our condition! Now there is sufficient foundation for peace and safety to those exercised with such fears, and brought into such dangers. But Christ is a refuge in all trouble; there is a foundation for rational support and peace in him, whatever threatens us. He, whose heart is fixed, trusting in Christ, need not be afraid of any evil tidings. "As the mountains are round about Jerusalem, so Christ is round about them that fear him."

JONATHAN EDWARDS

THE HOLY SPIRIT OF PROMISE

1 JOHN 4:13 NIV

We know that we live in him and he in us,
because he has given us of his Spirit.

Jesus told how this dispensation of the Holy Spirit would begin: "I tell you the truth: It is for your good that I am going away. Unless I go away, the Counselor will not come to you; but if I go, I will send him to you" (John 16:7).

The fulfillment of Christ's critical promise to His disciples came to them in John 20:21–22. The resurrected Jesus breathed on the disciples and told them to "receive the Holy Spirit." He then filled them in a far more powerful expression at Pentecost in Acts 2:1–4. These glorious events unleashed a new revolutionary economy of the Holy Spirit for the "Church Age" and onward until the return of Christ.

The Holy Spirit now indwells every person who receives Christ as his or her personal Savior (Romans 8:9). Oh, that we would absorb the magnitude of that spiritual revolution! Dear believer in Christ, the Spirit of the living God—the Spirit of Jesus Christ Himself, the Spirit of Truth—dwells inside of you!

BETH MOORE

SURROUNDED BY MIRACLES

PSALM 139:7 NASB
Where can I go from Your Spirit?
Or where can I flee from Your presence?

In fact, it is the normality not the uniqueness of God's miracles that causes them to be so staggering. Rather than shocking the globe with an occasional demonstration of deity, God has opted to display his power daily. Proverbially. Pounding waves. Prism-cast colors. Birth, death, life. We are surrounded by miracles. God is throwing testimonies at us like fireworks, each one exploding, "God is! God is!"

The psalmist marveled at such holy handiwork. "Where can I go from your Spirit?" he questioned with delight. "Where can I flee from your presence? If I go up to the heavens, you are there; if I make my bed in the depths, you are there." . . .

Would you like to see Jesus? Do you dare be an eyewitness of His Majesty? Then rediscover amazement.

The next time you hear a baby laugh or see an ocean wave, take note. Pause and listen as His Majesty whispers ever so gently, "I'm here."

MAX LUCADO

WHERE TWO OR THREE ARE GATHERED

MATTHEW 18:20 NLT
*"For where two or three gather together
because they are mine,
I am there among them."*

Our Lord has deigned to give us a great assurance, beloved brethren, when He says in the Gospel: "Where two or three are gathered together for my sake, there am I in the midst of them." If He condescends to be present among two or three, how much more so when all the people are gathered in church with pious devotion, the body of the Church united with Christ its Head in a society of harmonious members? "Where two or three," He says, "are gathered together for my sake" Now since a congregation pertains to many people, we must perceive how the Divine Word has judged that we should talk about two or three. I believe that it can be said about one individual, because he can be collected in the house of God, that is, in order to pray to God a man should enter wholly, not only with the exterior senses, but also the interior ones, with holy desires, faith, and good works.

CAESARIUS OF ARLES

PRACTICING GOD'S PRESENCE

EXODUS 33:14 NKJV
*And He said, "My Presence will go with you,
and I will give you rest."*

We should never leave our prayer closets in the morning without having concentrated our thoughts deeply and intensely on the fact of the actual presence of God there with us, encompassing us, and filling the room as literally as it fills heaven itself. It may not lead to any distinct results at first, but, as we make repeated efforts to realize the presence of God, it will become increasingly real to us. And, as the habit grows upon us, when alone in a room, or when treading the award of some natural woodland temple, or when pacing the stony street—in the silence of night, or amid the teeming crowds of daylight—we shall often find ourselves whispering the words, "Thou art near; thou art here, O Lord."

F. B. MEYER

VICTORY IN CHRIST

2 CORINTHIANS 2:14 NIV
*But thanks be to God, who always leads us
in triumphal procession in Christ and
through us spreads everywhere the fragrance
of the knowledge of him.*

This passage implies that God always leads us in triumph provided we stay in Christ. This raises questions: Aren't Christians often defeated? Do they not often go down in disaster? The answer is no, not if they stay "in Christ," for staying in Christ is the victory. When you stay in Him you manifest a spirit which cannot be defeated, for the manifestation of that spirit is the victory.

Jesus went down in defeat at the cross, but at the very moment of defeat he manifested a spirit which was the victory: "Father, forgive them; for they know not what they do." That spirit was the victory amid defeat. So if you manifest His spirit amid your defeat, you are led in triumph—for that spirit is the victory, the victory that overcomes the world! When a Roman persecutor said to a Christian who was in the tyrant's grip, "What can your Master do for you now?" The man replied, "He can help me to forgive you." That forgiveness was the victory!

E. STANLEY JONES

JESUS' LAST COMMAND

MATTHEW 28:19–20 NRSV
"Go therefore and make disciples of all nations,
baptizing them in the name of the Father and
of the Son and of the Holy Spirit, . . . And remember, I
am with you always, to the end of the age."

It was not an unfair command. The Old Testament foreshadowed it. Jesus' daily teaching anticipated it. His frequent prejudice-free ministry among both Samaritans and Gentiles had given the disciples a real-life demonstration of how to carry it out. Now He added the promise of His own authority bequeathed and His own presence in company—if they obeyed!

Still later, moments before He ascended back into heaven from the Mount of Olives (near Bethany), He added a further promise: "You will receive power when the Holy Spirit comes on you; and you will be my witnesses. . . ." Then followed Jesus' famous formula for the exocentric progression of the gospel: ". . . in Jerusalem, and in all Judea and Samaria, *and to the ends of the earth*" (Acts 1:8, italics added).

It was Jesus' last command. Without another word, and without waiting for any discussion of the proposal, He ascended into heaven to await His followers' complete obedience to it!

DON RICHARDSON

EQUIPPED FOR GOD'S WORK

MATTHEW 28:20 ESV
*"And behold, I am with you always,
to the end of the age."*

Every ambassador expects to be supplied with all that he needs for his embassy. "He who hath sent me is with me. The Father hath not left me alone." That word tells us how the Father was always with the Son, the source of strength and comfort. Even so the Church of Christ in her mission: "Go ye and teach all nations" has the promise. "Lo, I am with you alway." The believer need never hold back because of deficiency. The Lord does not demand anything which He does not give the power to perform. Every believer may depend on it, that as the Father gave His Holy Spirit to the Son to equip Him for His work, so the Lord Jesus will give His people all they need. The grace to demonstrate Christ . . . is given to everyone who only heartily and believingly takes up his heavenly calling. The sender cares for all that is needful for the sent ones.

ANDREW MURRAY

THE UNFINISHED DRAMA

MARK 16:6 NASB

And he said to them, "Do not be amazed;
you are looking for Jesus the Nazarene,
who has been crucified. He has risen; He is not here;
behold, here is the place where they laid Him."

In the Christian community we have passed on the unfinished drama of God. . . . Act VI is where we fit in, formed by what we have learned in the preceding parts. Immersed in the meta-narrative, the grand story of the people of God—the commandments, goals, chronicles, poetry, warnings, promises, and songs of the entire Revelation—we are formed to act with the character of God's people, imitating the virtues and deeds of God himself. And we have a great advantage, for, as we improvise Act VI in keeping with the spirit of the rest of the drama, we know that the Author is still alive!

What a great gift this meta-narrative is! It offers the people of the world around us a story into which they can place themselves and find forgiveness for their past, purpose for their present, and hope for their future.

MARVA DAWN

THE READMITTED CHRIST

REVELATION 3:20 NIV
*"Here I am! I stand at the door and knock.
If anyone hears my voice and opens the door, I will
come in and eat with him, and he with me."*

The greatest invitation in the Bible is contained in
Revelation 3:20:

"Here I am! I stand at the door and knock. If anyone
hears my voice and opens the door, I will come in and eat
with him, and he with me." . . .

Notice that this invitation is extended to the last church
ever mentioned in the Bible. That fact grips me with
urgency for our day.

G. Campbell Morgan said: "The only cure for lukewarmness is the readmission of the excluded Christ.
Apostasy must be confronted with His fidelity, looseness
with conviction born of His authority, poverty with the
fact of His wealth, frost with the mighty fire of His enthusiasm, and death with the life divine that is in His gift.
There is no other cure for the malady of the world, for
the lukewarmness of the Church than the readmitted
Christ."

DAVID JEREMIAH

OUR GARDENER

MARK 4:26–27 NLT

Jesus also said, "Here is another illustration of what the Kingdom of God is like: A farmer planted seeds in a field, and then he went on with his other activities. As the days went by, the seeds sprouted and grew without the farmer's help."

E very moment—literally, every time the eye twinkles—God is watering us. We have become so accustomed to it that we hardly realize how much we owe to it. Sometimes by the gentle distillation of dew that gathers almost imperceptibly on our spirits, and we hardly know whence or how it has come. Sometimes by the touch of a moistening sponge, applied by the very hand of God. Sometimes by a shower of grace. By a text suggested to our memory; a holy thought; the look, or act, or word of some companion; a paragraph in a paper; a sentence in a book—God waters us, and we become fresh and green, where the leaf showed signs of becoming shriveled and sere.

How blessed is life like this! In such hands—watched and guarded by such care—nurtured with such tenderness! May the result in each of us be—not the disappointment of wild grapes, but—the abundant clusters that will make glad the great Husbandman of our souls.

F. B. MEYER

ABOUT HIS LOVE
FOR YOU

*But God shows his love for us
in that while we were still sinners,
Christ died for us.*

ROMANS 5:8 ESV

ABOUT HIS LOVE FOR YOU

Love doesn't settle for the moment. Love refuses to be limited by time. It makes promises about the future. Lovers declare vows. Love wants to be counted on for right now and for tomorrow, too. Everything we understand about love flows from the Grand Lover, God Himself. Truly, we love because He first loved us.

If love makes promises, then God makes promises. And God's love has the astonishing quality of timelessness. Not only can He declare His eternal love for us, He can also assure us that He has always loved us. Human lovers promise fidelity until the stars fall; God tells us He was already in love with us when He made the stars.

Every one of God's promises has its root in God's love, but those you are about to think about focus directly on the infinite and over-whelming qualities of His love toward us.

GOD'S LOVE FOR THE WORLD

JOHN 3:16 NIV

"For God so loved the world that he gave his one and only Son, that whoever believes in him shall not perish but have eternal life."

The Jew was ready enough to think of God as loving Israel, but no passage appears to be cited in which any Jewish writer maintains that God loved the world. It is a distinctively Christian idea that God's love is wide enough to embrace all mankind. His love is not confined to any national group or any spiritual elite. . . . John tells us that His love is shown in the gift of His Son. Of this gift Odeberg finely says, "the Son is God's gift to the world, and, moreover, it is *the* gift. There are no Divine gifts apart from or outside the one-born (sic) Son." In typical Johannine fashion "gave" is used in two senses. God gave the Son by sending Him into the world, but God also gave the Son on the cross. Notice that the cross is not said to show us the love of the Son (as in Galatians 2.20), but that of the Father.

LEON MORRIS

THE UNCONQUERABLE LOVE OF GOD

ROMANS 8:38–39 NIV

For I am convinced that neither death nor life,
neither angels nor demons, neither the present
nor the future, nor any powers, . . . will be able
to separate us from the love of God. . . .

Here we pass from human temptations to superhuman trials. . . . Even with all the forces of the enemy ranged against us, nothing can separate us from the love of God.

Death here refers primarily to the death which separates the soul from the love of God, rather than what we usually think of as death, which merely separates the soul from the body. *Life* here presumably refers to the life of sin, which is constantly trying to separate us from the love of God.

Angels and principalities must refer to the devil and his hosts, against whom we have to struggle. Things *present* are the desires of this world, and *things to come* are the trials and temptations which may yet afflict us in this life. The powers are spiritual beings rather like angels, who must, however, be distinguished from them. They also fight to separate us from the love of God, but they cannot prevail if that love is rooted and grounded in us.

ORIGEN

THE LOVE OF GOD DRAWS US

"For God so loved the world that he gave his only Son, so that everyone who believes in him will not perish but have eternal life."

We must be persuaded how much God loved us so that we don't shrink from Him in despair. And we need to be shown also what kind of people we are whom He loved so that we also don't withdraw from Him out of pride. But He dealt with us so that we could profit from His strength, and, in the weakness of humility, our holiness could be perfected. One of the Psalms implies this. It says, "Thou, O God, didst send a spontaneous rain, whereby Thou didst make Thine inheritance perfect, when it was weary." The "spontaneous rain" is grace given freely and not according to merit. He didn't give it because we were worthy, but because He willed. Knowing this, we shouldn't trust in ourselves. That is what is meant by being made "weak." However, He perfects us and says to the Apostle Paul, "My grace is sufficient for thee, for my strength is made perfect in weakness."

AUGUSTINE

THE MOTHERHOOD OF GOD

2 CORINTHIANS 1:3-4 NIV
*Praise be to the God and Father of our
Lord Jesus Christ, the Father of compassion
and the God of all comfort.*

In God there is the mother-nature as well as the Father-hood. All love was first in Him, ere it was lit up in human hearts. The fires that burn so brightly on the altars of motherhood the world over, were lit in the first instance from the Heart of God; and He keeps them alight. And therefore the love that is so quick to detect and so swift to hush the wail of the babe; which is so sensitive to discover that something ails the troubled heart; which is so inventive of little methods of solace, now by tender touch, and again by delicate suggestion—this love is in the great heart of God, and awaits our need to enwrap us in the embrace of an infinite sympathy and comfort. . . .

Few have suffered more than [Paul] did, from the moment that he gave up all for Christ, to the hour in which he died a martyr for the faith . . . And yet he said, *God comforteth us.*

F. B. MEYER

THE WORD MADE FLESH

ROMANS 5:6–8 ESV

For while we were still weak, at the right time Christ died for the ungodly. For one will scarcely die for a righteous person—though perhaps for a good person one would dare even to die—but God shows his love for us in that while we were still sinners, Christ died for us.

What a magnificent mystery of the Word Made Flesh! Christ, the power that created the universe, relinquished all power to come to us as one of us, mortal, human, walking the short road from the womb to the tomb. Often we stumble along, not knowing where we're going, but understanding that the journey is worth it because Jesus took it for us, shared it with us. Because the immortal God became mortal, we all share in the immortality as well as the mortality. And how can we begin to understand our immortality until we accept our mortality?

What I believe is so magnificent, so glorious, that it is beyond finite comprehension. To believe that the universe was created by a purposeful, benign Creator is one thing. To believe that this Creator took on human vesture, accepted death and mortality, was tempted, betrayed, broken, and all for love of us, defies reason.

MADELEINE L'ENGLE

JOY IN THE CHRISTIAN LIFE

GALATIANS 5:22 NIV

But the fruit of the Spirit is love, joy, peace,
patience, kindness, goodness, faithfulness . . .

Christians, then, can be the happiest people in the world despite trying circumstances. Charles Spurgeon described well the joy that filled his own soul: "When the Lord first pardoned my sin, I was so joyous that I could scarcely refrain from dancing. . . . But it is not only at the beginning of the Christian life that believers have a reason to sing; as long as they live they discover reasons to sing about the ways of the Lord, and their experiences of His constant loving-kindness lead them to say, 'I will extol the LORD at all times; His praise will always be on my lips.'"

At the same time, Christians caught up in hypocrisy or rebellion can be genuinely miserable people. For them, experiencing the very real joys of righteous living is at best a faded memory.

With all these things in mind, "how then should we live?" Not as hypocrites but rather as forgiven sinners depending daily upon the Holy Spirit's power in every aspect of our lives.

TIMOTHY GEORGE AND JOHN WOODBRIDGE

GOD-GIVEN LOVE

MATTHEW 10:29 NIV
"Are not two sparrows sold for a penny?
Yet not one of them will fall to the ground
apart from the will of your Father."

I learned to love the four plain walls of a house when I had to live for a number of months without any. . . . Some primitive peoples, including the Indians with whom I was living, like togetherness enough to live without walls. Some presumably civilized peoples are getting to like it more and more, but it seems to me an uncivilized idea. Togetherness is all very well in certain very limited circumstances—in a family, for instance, up to a point. But even there it won't work unless there is God-given love.

The love that comes from God is the only kind that properly minds the gaps. His love appreciates distinctions, respects privacy, and recognizes the variety which he has put into his marvelous world, variety which makes for excitement and fun. Who doesn't like to watch people, to study the differences in faces, behavior, dress, and speech? Isn't variety a part of the joy of collecting things like shells or rocks, or of studying astronomy, botany, ornithology?

ELISABETH ELLIOT

PERFECT CONTENTMENT

1 JOHN 5:11 NASB
*And the testimony is this, that God has given
us eternal life, and this life is in His Son.*

The joy of the Lord in the spirit springs also from *an
assurance that all the future, whatever it may be, is guaranteed by divine goodness,* that being children of God, the love
of God towards us is not of a mutable character, but abides
and remains unchangeable. The believer feels an entire
satisfaction in leaving himself in the hands of eternal and
immutable love. . . . If my salvation be still a matter of hazard and jeopardy, unmingled joy is not mine, and deep
peace is still out of my reach. But when I know that he
whom I have rested in hath power and grace enough to
complete that which he hath begun in me, and for
me; when I see the work of Christ to be no halfway
redemption, but a complete and eternal salvation; when
I perceive that the promises are established upon an unchangeable basis, and are yea and amen in Christ Jesus,
ratified by oath and sealed by blood, then my soul hath
perfect contentment.

C. H. SPURGEON

REMEMBER GOD'S GOODNESS

PSALM 9:10 NKJV
*And those who know Your name will put their trust
in You; for You, LORD, have not forsaken
those who seek You.*

The deep and precious truths that God has brought to me over the years and even just yesterday seem a thousand miles away. It doesn't happen every morning, but enough to make it an ongoing reality. And I know I am not alone in this. . . .

Virtually every person I've ever counseled follows a similar pattern. Over the course of our time together, some wonderful things begin to happen. Not necessarily at first, and never on command, but God shows up. The lights turn on for these people; their heart is lifted; grateful tears flow. Suddenly, faith, hope, and love seem the only way to live. And I nearly dread the next session. When they return the following week, it is as though it never happened. The marvelous day is a distant memory. Life is hard, God is distant, and love is foolish. . . . I want to grab them and shake them into sense, shouting, "Don't you *remember?* Why did you let it slip away?" Wisdom has kept me restrained so far.

JOHN ELDREDGE

DAY 300

GOD LOVES THE WORLD

2 CORINTHIANS 5:18–19 NASB
*Now all these things are from God, who
reconciled us to Himself through Christ and gave
us the ministry of reconciliation, namely, that God
was in Christ reconciling the world to Himself,
not counting their trespasses against them, and He
has committed to us the word of reconciliation.*

Look, God loves the whole world. You see it in common grace. You see it in compassion. You see it in warning. And you see it in the offer of the gospel. And Jesus is the Savior of the whole world. He is designated as the Savior of the whole world. He is called the Savior of the whole world. The atoning work of Christ, the work of Christ on the cross is identifying Himself as the Savior of the world has implications to the whole world. And it was designed to reveal God's universal love for sinners— the whole guilty human race. Because of the work of Jesus Christ on the cross as the Savior of the world, all sinners are called to repent and to believe and to be forgiven, and if they are refused they are guilty and they will be punished. And they have spurned the love of God . . . the love of God is to the whole world. And that is the first and essential establishing principle.

JOHN MACARTHUR

328   HIS PROMISES

LOVE THAT WILL NOT LET YOU GO

1 JOHN 4:16 ESV
*God is love, and whoever abides in love abides in God,
and God abides in him.*

Have you noticed how love in this world is fickle? People talk about love, but oh, is it fickle. We're not talking about that kind of love, questioning whether it even is love. There's a lovely hymn written by George Mathison called, "O Love That Will Not Let Me Go." There's a sad story behind that hymn. George Mathison, the writer, was to marry the love of his life. When he announced to her that he felt God's call to missionary service, she said, "I don't want to be a missionary," and left him, refusing to marry. All alone he wrote these words, "O love that will not let me go, I rest my weary soul in Thee, I give Thee back the life I owe that in Thine ocean depths its flow may richer, fuller be." God loves you this much. Can you say with Mathison, I give Thee back the life I owe to such love that in Thine ocean depths its flow may richer, fuller be? That's the question.

JOHN MACARTHUR

ANCIENT LOVE

JEREMIAH 31:3 NLT

Long ago the LORD said to Israel: "I have loved you,
my people, with an everlasting love.
With unfailing love I have drawn you to myself."

Meditate upon the love of Christ to you. *It is a love ancient and venerable, tried and proved.* He loved you when you were not; he loved you when you were, but were not what you should be. . . . He loved you so as to suffer and to die, and he loves you so as to permit you to suffer for his sake. He has loved you so well as to bear with your ill manners, your shortcomings, and your transgressions, your coldness, your backsliding, your lack of prayer, your hardness of heart, your little love to your brethren, and all the other sins of which I will not now accuse you, for it is a time of love. He has loved you right on without pausing or slackening. Some of you have known his love these twenty, thirty, forty, fifty years; yes, some of you even more than that. It is no new thing with us to sing, "Jesus loves me." All this while he has never failed us once, nor done us an ill turn.

C. H. SPURGEON

ABOUT
ETERNAL
LIFE

---

*"For this is the will of My Father,
that everyone who beholds the Son and
believes in Him will have eternal life, and
I Myself will raise him up on the last day."*

JOHN 6:40 NASB

ABOUT ETERNAL LIFE

All human promises have a time stamp. We can't promise beyond this life. Even the bonds of marriage are limited to "until death do us part." Only God can make promises beyond time. Only God can promise us eternal life. Because of the source, God's timeless promises can invade time. Jesus made a startling announcement: "I assure you, those who listen to my message and believe in God who sent me have eternal life. They will never be condemned for their sins, but they have already passed from death into life" (John 5:24 NLT). In Christ, our possession of eternal life is now, not then. The real problem and threat of death has passed.

Consider carefully whether or not you have taken hold of Jesus as you read these thoughts on God's eternal life promises. You can have eternal life today.

THE FINAL HOUR

JOHN 10:28 NRSV
"I give them eternal life, and they will never perish.
No one will snatch them out of my hand."

It is the hour of your dying. You are in the hospital. It is the middle of the night. . . . Long ago you had heard the voice of the Lord and you obeyed and followed him in faith. But now a storm begins to rage as Satan throws all his final force against your faith. You feel the reality of eternity like you have never felt it before. The wind of doubt and the waves of fear lash your soul. And then, by the grace of God, there comes a scene and it is your scene. You are in a boat in a storm. And Jesus is approaching you on the water. And on his face there is no fear. With his hair and his cloak flying in the wind, he stops a short way off and stands with his strong hands relaxed at his side in sovereign peace. And from the boat . . . you say, "Christ, bid me come!" And he says, "Come." And you begin to walk on the water.

JOHN PIPER

FACE TO FACE WITH GOD

JOHN 10:28 NIV
*"I give them eternal life, and they shall never perish;
no one can snatch them out of my hand."*

There is a long tradition which promises that the final hope of God's sons and daughters is to live face to face in the Father's presence. . . . We wait for that final moment of unity because we have confidence, already knowing who God is and what he is about. He is like the abrasive power and suffering vulnerability of Jesus of Nazareth. We already know who he is, for whoever has seen the Son has seen the Father. In his *crucifixion of solidarity* with us and in his *resurrection of surprising newness,* we know two things. We know what is promised to us, because what he has done is what he will do. And we know what is asked of us, for we are called to share in his vision and in his work. And knowing those two things is enough. It is enough as a context in which we keep risky covenant with the utterly faithful one.

WALTER BRUEGGEMAN

OUR GLORIOUS INHERITANCE

I PETER 1:3-4 NIV

In his great mercy he has given us new birth into
a living hope through the resurrection of Jesus Christ
from the dead, and into an inheritance that can never
perish, spoil or fade—kept in heaven for you.

God of my forefathers, I cry unto You. You have been the refuge of good and wise people in every generation. When history began, You were the first enlightener of minds, and Yours was the Spirit that first led them out of their brutish estate and made them human. Through all the ages You have been the Lord and giver of life, the source of all knowledge, the fountain of all goodness.

The patriarchs trusted You and were not put to shame:

The prophets sought You and You committed Your word to their lips:

. . . The apostles waited upon You and they were filled with Your Holy Spirit:

The martyrs called upon You and You were with them in the midst of the flame:

Forbid it, Holy Lord, that I should fail to profit by these great memories of the ages that are gone by, or to enter into the glorious inheritance which You have prepared for me; through Jesus Christ my Lord. Amen.

JOHN BAILLIE

ETERNAL LIFE

PSALM 91:16 NIV
*With long life will I satisfy him
and show him my salvation.*

Jesus Christ came into the world to destroy death, and we can say with Paul, if we will, "Oh, death, where is thy sting?" And we can hear a voice rolling down from heaven saying, "Buried in the bosom of the Son of God." He took death unto His own bosom. He went into the grave to conquer and overthrow it, and when He arose from the dead said, "Because I live, ye shall live also." Thank God, we have a long life with Christ in glory.

My dear friends, if we are in Christ we are never going to die. Do you believe that? If sometime you should read that D. L. Moody, of East Northfield, is dead, don't believe a word of it. He has gone up higher, that is all; gone out of this old clay tenement into a house that is immortal, a body that death cannot touch, that sin cannot taint, a body fashioned like unto His own glorious body.

DWIGHT L. MOODY

HOLD TIGHTLY TO CHRIST

MATTHEW 10:22 NIV
*"All men will hate you because of me,
but he who stands firm to the end will be saved."*

Why did Christ urge His disciples to take up the cross and follow Him? . . . With respect to the suffering He would experience and His disciples would endure, He suggests, "For whosoever will save his life, shall lose it; and whosoever will lose his life, shall find it." And because His disciples must suffer for His sake, Christ said to them, "Behold, I send you prophets and wise men and scribes; and some of them ye shall kill and crucify." . . . As a result, He gave them this encouragement: "Fear not them which kill the body, but are not able to kill the soul; but rather fear Him who is able to send both soul and body into hell." He urged them to hold tightly to their professions of faith in Him. For He promised to confess before His Father those who confess His name before men. But He announced that He would deny those who deny Him and would be ashamed of those who were ashamed to confess allegiance to Him.

IRENAEUS

THE POWER OF DEATH IS GONE

1 CORINTHIANS 15:20 NIV
*But Christ has indeed been raised from the dead,
the firstfruits of those who have fallen asleep.*

Death is destroyed. The cross has triumphed over it. It no longer has any power but is truly dead. This is why all of Christ's disciples despise death and no longer fear it. They take the offensive against it. And by the sign of the cross and by faith in Christ, they trample it down as dead. Before the Savior came, death was terrible to the saints. Everyone wept for the dead as though they perished. But now that the Savior has risen, death isn't terrible anymore. For everyone who believes in Christ tramples over death. They would rather die than deny their faith in Christ. For they know that when they die they aren't destroyed but actually begin to live. Through the Resurrection they become incorruptible. For the devil, who once maliciously rejoiced in death, is the only one truly dead now that we are relieved of death's pains.

ATHANASIUS

SAFETY AND SALVATION IN JESUS

JOHN 3:36 ESV
Whoever believes in the Son has eternal life;
whoever does not obey the Son shall not see life,
but the wrath of God remains on him.

Jesus, Lover of my soul,
 Let me to thy bosom fly,
While the nearer waters roll,
While the tempest still is high:
Hide me, O my Savior, hide,
Till the storm of life be past!
Safe into the haven guide,
Oh, receive my soul at last!

Plenteous grace with thee is found,
Grace to cover all my sin,
Let the healing streams abound;
Make and keep me pure within:
Thou of life the fountain art,
Freely let me take of thee,
Spring thou up within my heart,
Rise to all eternity.

CHARLES WESLEY

THE WONDROUS CROSS

GALATIANS 6:14 ESV

*But far be it from me to boast except in the cross
of our Lord Jesus Christ, by which the world
has been crucified to me, and I to the world.*

When I survey the wondrous Cross
  Where the young Prince of Glory died,
My richest gain I count but loss,
And pour contempt on all my pride.

Forbid it, Lord, that I should boast
Save in the death of Christ, my God;
All the vain things that charm me most,
I sacrifice them to his blood.

See from his head, his hands, his feet,
Sorrow and love flow mingled down;
Did e'er such love and sorrow meet?
Or thorns compose so rich a crown?

Were the whole realm of nature mine,
That were a present far too small;
Love so amazing, so divine,
Demands my soul, my life, my all.

ISSAC WATTS

THE NEW CREATION

REVELATION 21:5 NLT
*And the one sitting on the throne said,
"Look, I am making all things new!"
And then he said to me, "Write this down,
for what I tell you is trustworthy and true."*

The silence of God in Revelation is broken by his
declaration, "Behold, I make all things new." The
throne upon which God sits symbolizes his sovereignty
and majesty. It is from this position of awesome power
that he announces his intention of creating the new order.
The renovation of the universe was a familiar concept in
apocalyptic literature. . . . Through the prophet Isaiah
God had promised, "For behold, I create new heavens
and a new earth; and the former things shall not be
remembered or come into mind" (Isaiah 65:17). The
transformation which Paul saw taking place in the lives of
believers will have its counterpart on a cosmic scale when
a totally new order will replace the old order marred
by sin.

ROBERT H. MOUNCE

HE WILL REMOVE OUR SORROWS

REVELATION 21:4 NLT

*"He will remove all of their sorrows, and there will
be no more death or sorrow or crying or pain.
For the old world and its evils are gone forever."*

The "cup of sorrows" and the "cup of joys" cannot be separated. Jesus knew this, even though in the midst of his anguish in the garden, when his soul was "sorrowful to the point of death" (Matthew 26:38), he needed an angel from heaven to remind him of it. Our cup is often so full of pain that joy seems completely unreachable. When we are crushed like grapes, we cannot think of the wine we will become. The sorrow overwhelms us, makes us throw ourselves on the ground, face down, and sweat drops of blood. Then we need to be reminded that our cup of sorrow is also our cup of joy and that one day we will be able to taste the joy as fully as we now taste the sorrow.

HENRI NOUWEN

LIFE WITHOUT LIMIT

JOHN 17:3 NRSV
"And this is eternal life, that they may know you, the only true God, and Jesus Christ whom you have sent."

Because God's nature is infinite, everything that flows out of it is infinite also. We poor human creatures are constantly being frustrated by limitations imposed upon us from without and within. The days of the years of our lives are few, and swifter than a weaver's shuttle. Life is a short and fevered rehearsal for a concert we cannot stay to give. . . .

How completely satisfying to turn from our limitations to a God who has none. . . . The gift of eternal life in Christ Jesus is as limitless as God. The Christian man possesses God's own life and shares His infinitude with Him. In God there is life enough for all and time enough to enjoy it. Whatever is possessed of natural life runs through its cycle from birth to death and ceases to be, but the life of God returns upon itself and ceases never. And this is life eternal: to know the only true God, and Jesus Christ whom He has sent.

A. W. TOZER

UNEQUAL PAY

ROMANS 8:16–17 NIV

*The Spirit himself testifies with our spirit that
we are God's children. Now if we are children,
then we are heirs—heirs of God and co-heirs
with Christ, if indeed we share in his sufferings
in order that we may also share in his glory.*

It is clear that the bottom line is that the reward we
receive will not be equal pay for equal service. Rather,
our reward will be a hundred times greater than any work
we actually have done. God will pay the legalist who has
worked for a fixed price, but in the end He will compensate far beyond expectations those who have trusted
Him. Our relationship with Him is not just between master and slave, but between a Father who delights in sharing His inheritance and His obedient child.

In the end we shall receive much more than we have
merited; in fact, as we have already learned, we "deserve"
nothing. God will give us rewards that are totally out of
proportion to the work we have done. Since no one
"earns" rewards anyway, we shall receive the benefits of a
gracious wage. We will have hearts of gratitude for all of
eternity.

ERWIN LUTZER

THE ASCENDED CHRIST

PHILIPPIANS 3:20 NLT
*But we are citizens of heaven, where the
Lord Jesus Christ lives. And we are eagerly
waiting for him to return as our Savior.*

Since, then, you have been raised with Christ, set your hearts on things above, where Christ is seated at the right hand of God. Set your minds on things above, not on earthly things" (Colossians 3:1–2). With these words, Paul stresses the need for a *right perspective on life*. It is very easy for the believer, like anyone else, to get trapped in a rut. Work, family responsibilities, financial anxieties—all can become burdens that make us tired and weary. We look ahead and see only more of the same sort of thing confronting us. It is very demoralizing. But it is here that Paul has some vital advice. Look upward! Raise your head up, and look to the skies. Christ has ascended, blazing a trail in which we can follow. Thinking about the Ascension is a helpful way of making sure that our outlook on life is right. It helps us recall that our destiny does not lie on this earth but with the ascended Christ, who has gone ahead of us.

ALISTER E. McGRATH

TAKE UP YOUR CROSS

MATTHEW 16:24 NIV

Then Jesus said to his disciples, "If anyone
would come after me, he must deny himself
and take up his cross and follow me."

It is as though Jesus said to them, "You still confess me
to be the Messiah? You still wish to follow me? If so,
you should realise quite clearly where I am going, and
understand that, by following me, you will be going there
too." . . .

The sight of a man being taken to the place of public
crucifixion was not unfamiliar in the Roman world of
that day. Such a man was commonly made to carry the
crossbeam, the *patibulum,* of his cross as he went to his
death. That is the picture which Jesus' words would con-
jure up in the minds of his hearers. If they were not prepared for that outcome to their discipleship, let them
change their minds while there was time—but let them
first weigh the options in the balances of the kingdom of
God: "for whoever would save his life will lose it; and
whoever loses his life for my sake and the gospel's will save
it" (Mark 8:35).

F. F. BRUCE

BLESSED ASSURANCE

1 PETER 1:3–4 NLT
*Now we live with a wonderful expectation because
Jesus Christ rose again from the dead. For God has
reserved a priceless inheritance for his children.*

Blessed assurance, Jesus is mine!
O what a foretaste of glory divine!
Heir of salvation, purchase of God,
Born of His Spirit, washed in His blood.

*This is my story, this is my song,
Praising my Savior all the day long;
This is my story, this is my song,
Praising my Savior all the day long.*

Perfect submission—all is at rest,
I in my Savior am happy and blest;
Watching and waiting, looking above,
Filled with His goodness, lost in His love.

FANNY CROSBY

WE SHALL REST

REVELATION 14:13 NLT

And I heard a voice from heaven saying,
"Write this down: Blessed are those who die in
the Lord from now on. Yes, says the Spirit, they
are blessed indeed, for they will rest from all their
toils and trials; for their good deeds follow them!"

That which makes everything laborious here is sin—
the opposition of Satan and the world, and the drag
of our old nature. . . . But when we die in the Lord, we
shall rest from this labor. Satan's work will be clean done.
. . . No more any flesh—all spirit, all new man; no more
any weight or drag—we shall rest from our labors. Oh, it
is this makes death in the Lord blessed! We shall not rest
from all work; we shall be as the angels of God—we shall
serve Him day and night in His temple. We shall not rest
from our work, but from our labors. There will be no toil,
no pain, in our work. We shall rest in our work. Oh, let
this make you willing to depart, and make death look
pleasant, and heaven a home. "We shall rest from our
labors." It is the world of holy love, where we shall give
free, full, unfettered, unwearied expression to our love for
ever.

ROBERT MURRAY MCCHEYNE

THE NEW NATURE OF DEATH

ROMANS 8:10 NIV

But if Christ is in you, your body is dead because of sin, yet your spirit is alive because of righteousness.

The nature, then, of death, is changed to believers by Jesus Christ, so that "the day of their death is better than the day of their birth." Death to them is no more a curse, but a blessing, which puts an end to their sins and troubles, causing them to pass to perfect holiness and happiness, and from being absent from the Lord to carry them into His presence in paradise. From being strangers on the earth, it introduces them into their heavenly inheritance. From their wanderings and agitations here below, it brings them into the haven of everlasting rest. . . . Death is the passage of Jordan by which believers enter the heavenly Canaan. In order that its waves may not overwhelm them in passing, Jesus Christ arrests them, since He is in His people and consequently with them. This was David's support, "Though I walk through the valley of the shadow of death, I will fear no evil; for Thou art with me."

ROBERT HALDANE

SELF-DENIAL

GALATIANS 2:20 NLT

I myself no longer live, but Christ lives in me.
So I live my life in this earthly body by trusting in the
Son of God, who loved me and gave himself for me.

I f any man will *come after* me, let him deny himself, take up his cross, and *follow me.*" This word not only gives us the will but also the power for self-denial. He who does not simply wish to reach heaven through Christ, but comes after Him for His own sake, will *follow* Him. And in his heart Jesus takes the place that self had. . . . The undivided surrender to follow Him is crowned with this wonderful blessing, that Christ by His Spirit becomes his life. Christ's spirit of self-denying love is poured out upon him, and to deny self is the greatest joy of his heart, and the means of the deepest communion with God. Self-denial is no longer a work for attaining perfection for himself. Nor is it merely a negative victory, of which the main feature is keeping self in check. Christ has taken the place of self, and His love and gentleness and kindness flow out to others, now that self is crucified.

ANDREW MURRAY

HIS PROMISES

THE LIFE GOD WILL GIVE

JAMES 1:12 NIV

Blessed is the man who perseveres under trial, because when he has stood the test, he will receive the crown of life that God has promised to those who love him.

The perfect life itself, which God will give, is the crown which we hope for. . . . Life—life with clearer vision than is possible to us in this world; life sensitive to more subtle and more ravishing harmonies; life with diviner buoyancy and vigour; life with more intense affections; life with wider horizons of thought; life with new and unhoped-for possibilities of righteousness; life with the capacity for closer friendships with the saintly spirits of the city of God; life with loftier raptures of adoration; life with profounder awe in the presence of God's majesty. . . .

The higher, larger, purer life is what we hope for, and this is what God has promised us. He promises it to those who love Him and who have endured temptation; for it is by the endurance of temptation in the power of love for Christ that the capacity for receiving that life in its amplest measure and noblest perfection is enlarged and perfected.

R. W. DALE

THE ULTIMATE SACRIFICE

PHILIPPIANS 3:8 NIV
*I consider everything a loss compared to the
surpassing greatness of knowing Christ Jesus my Lord,
for whose sake I have lost all things. I consider
them rubbish, that I may gain Christ.*

Central to New Testament teaching is the insistence that Christ's death is the ultimate sacrifice, provided by God to cleanse his people from the defilement of sin and consecrate them to himself in a relationship of heart-obedience. The victim and the priest of the new covenant are one, because Jesus offered perfect worship to the Father by a lifetime of obedience culminating in his death. . . .

His sacrifice on the cross, his entrance into the heavenly sanctuary, and his intercession for us, provide the only basis for relating to God under the new covenant. The whole life is to be lived in relation to the cross and to the sanctuary where Christ is enthroned as our crucified saviour and high priest. Indeed, it is ultimately our destiny to share with him in the fellowship of that heavenly or eschatological reality and to "serve him day and night in his temple" (see Revelation 7:15). Meanwhile, we worship God as we acknowledge these truths and respond to his mercies with grateful obedience.

DAVID PETERSON

True Worship

1 PETER 1:3–4 NKJV

Blessed be the God and Father of our Lord Jesus Christ, who according to His abundant mercy has begotten us again to a living hope through the resurrection of Jesus Christ from the dead, to an inheritance . . . reserved in heaven for you.

True worship is not about me. It is not about my knowledge, my experience, my healing, my empowerment. True worship proclaims and enacts the narrative of God's story. It is about the God of character, the God who is just, righteous, holy, merciful, and loving. It is about the God who acts, the God who creates a good world, the God who mourns over a world gone astray, the God who rescues the world—not by power but by weakness. It is about the God who cannot be contained in all the heavens, yet became contained in the womb of the Virgin Mary, born of her the Savior of the world. Worship is about the God who does for us what we cannot do for ourselves. It thankfully remembers how God became incarnate as the second Adam to reverse the human situation. He who knew no sin became one of us, and took on the consequence of our sin, death. By death he destroyed death, restored the nature of humanity, and opened the way to heaven.

ROBERT WEBBER

MAKING EVERYTHING NEW

REVELATION 21:5 NIV

He who was seated on the throne said, "I am
making everything new!" Then he said, "Write this
down, for these words are trustworthy and true."

It must be allowed that after all the researches we can
make, still our knowledge of the great truth which is
delivered to us in these words is exceedingly short and
imperfect. As this is a point of mere revelation, beyond
the reach of all our natural faculties, we cannot penetrate
far into it, nor form any adequate conception of it. But it
may be an encouragement to those who have in any
degree tasted of the powers of the world to come to go
as far as we can go, interpreting Scripture by Scripture,
according to the analogy of faith.

The Apostle, caught up in the visions of God, tells us
in the first verse of the chapter, "I saw a new heaven and
a new earth" and adds, (Revelation 21:5) "He that sat
upon the throne said," (I believe the only words which he
is said to utter throughout the whole book,) "Behold, I
make all things new."

JOHN WESLEY

ABOUT
HIS
RETURN

*He who is the faithful witness to all
these things says, "Yes, I am coming soon!"
Amen! Come, Lord Jesus!*

REVELATION 22:20 NLT

ABOUT HIS RETURN

The way we live our daily lives has a lot to do with how we understand Jesus' promises about His return. There's no mistaking the fact that He illustrated, taught, and insisted that those who follow Him will live each day aware that it might be the day of His return. This is not a reason to live frantically, but faithfully. Keeping faith with Jesus' promises about His return involves a dual attention on the commands for obedience and the commands to watch—action combined with attentiveness.

As you reflect on His promises to return, trace your schedule and thinking over the last few days. How much action and how much attentiveness have you exercised? Renew your intention to live an obedient life on the edge of your faith-seat.

THE WONDER OF THE BLESSED AGE

1 CORINTHIANS 2:9 NIV

*However, as it is written: "No eye has seen,
no ear has heard, no mind has conceived what
God has prepared for those who love him."*

The remarkable thing in the record of the Ages that have been, and that are, and that are going to be, is that each Age ends in apparent disaster. The saint alone knows . . . that these catastrophic occurrences are but incidental, and that a higher peace and a purer character are to be the permanent result. He knows that "this same Jesus," who trod this earth with naked feet, "and wrought with human hands the creeds of creeds," is coming again. . . . All that men have ever dreamed of Utopias and of Golden Ages will fade into foolish fancies beside the wonder of that blessed Age, that blessed period of Christ's reign among men. We have to remain stedfastly certain in Him, not go out of Him to see when He is coming; it is to be prophetic *living* as well as prophetic study. To the saint everything is instinct with the purpose of God. History is fulfilling prophecy all the time.

OSWALD CHAMBERS

VICTORY IN JESUS

REVELATION 5:13 ESV
*And I heard every creature in heaven and on
earth and under the earth and in the sea, and all
that is in them, saying, "To him who sits on the
throne and to the Lamb be blessing and honor
and glory and might forever and ever!"*

Like Hebrews, the Revelation to John focuses on the heavenly realm, where Jesus the crucified Messiah reigns in glory. The whole of life is to be lived in relation to the new Jerusalem and the victory of "the Lamb who was slain." From the point of view of those still on earth, the holy city must one day come down "out of heaven from God" (21:2). But confidence in the finished work of Jesus and his promises about the future is the way to share even now in the worship of heaven. Those who remain faithful to Jesus will enjoy the fruit of his victory in the full reality of his unshakable kingdom. Even those who feel overwhelmed by the powers ranged against them and who are persecuted for their faith should be moved by John's visions of heaven to live a life of joyful service to God in the present.

DAVID PETERSON

THE LORD IS COMING

ROMANS 2:6–8 ESV

He will render to each one according to his works: to those who by patience in well-doing seek for glory and honor and immortality, he will give eternal life; but for those who are self-seeking and do not obey the truth, but obey unrighteousness, there will be wrath and fury.

The good servant receives the bread of his labor with confidence. The lazy servant can't look his employer in the face. It is essential, therefore, that we be quick to practice good works, for of Him are all things. He warns us, "Behold, the Lord cometh, and His reward is before His face, to render to every man according to his work." He urges us, therefore, to attend to our work with a whole heart so that we won't be lazy in any good work. . . . Let us consider the whole multitude of His angels, how they always stand ready to serve His will. For the Scripture says, "Ten thousand times ten thousand stood around Him, and thousands of thousands ministered unto Him, and cried, 'Holy, holy, holy, is the Lord of Sabaoth; the whole creation is full of His glory.'" Let us, therefore, gather together in harmony and cry to Him earnestly as with one mouth, so that we can share in His great and glorious promises.

CLEMENT OF ROME

TRIUMPH

MATTHEW 25:23 ESV
His master said to him, "Well done, good and faithful servant. You have been faithful over a little; I will set you over much. Enter into the joy of your master."

Day of judgement, day of wonders!
Hark! the trumpet's awful sound,
Louder than a thousand thunders,
Shakes the vast creation round!
How the summons will the sinner's heart confound.

See the Judge, our nature wearing,
Cloth'd in majesty divine!
You who long for his appearing
Then shall say, "This God is mine!"
Gracious Saviour, own me in that day for thine!

Under sorrows and reproaches,
May this thought your courage raise.
Swiftly God's great day approaches,
Sighs shall then be chang'd to praise:
We shall triumph when the world is in a blaze.

JOHN NEWTON

TURN TO JESUS

*"Behold, I am coming soon! Blessed is he who
keeps the words of the prophecy in this book."*

Oh! ye people that today hear the words of Jesus! ye
are now this day invited to come to the mountain
of his church on which stands his cross and his throne. Ye
weary, heavy laden, sin-destroyed, sin-ruined souls; ye that
know and feel your need of Jesus; ye that weep because of
sin; ye are bidden to come now to Christ's cross, to look
to him who shed his blood for the ungodly, and looking
to him, you shall find peace and rest; so that when he
cometh with rainbow wreath and robes of storm, you
shall be able to see him not with alarm and terror, but
with joy and gladness. For you shall say, "Here he is, the
man who died for me has come to claim me, he who
bought me has come to receive me; my judge is my
Redeemer, and I will rejoice in him." Oh! turn ye . . .
turn ye unto God! . . . O Lord Jesus! by thy grace turn
every one of us to thyself!

C. H. SPURGEON

VICTORY

REVELATION 5:11–12 NIV

*Then I looked and heard the voice of many angels,
numbering thousands upon thousands, and ten thousand
times ten thousand. They encircled the throne and
the living creatures and the elders. In a loud voice
they sang: "Worthy is the Lamb, who was slain,
to receive power and wealth and wisdom and
strength and honor and glory and praise!"*

Let us pause and contemplate such a victory. Let us
picture to ourselves that celestial coronation scene.
Jesus our King seated on the throne of heaven, surrounded with glory, His kingdom universal, His enemies
under His feet, Satan vanquished, earthly magistrates and
potentates, sages and kings, armies and emperors, bowing
submissively before Him as King of Kings and Lord of
Lords; hymns of praise chanted by the heavenly choir;
tributes of adoration by the saints clothed in white; His
elect singing hallelujahs to Him that sitteth upon the
throne of God most high, and worshiping multitudes rais-
ing their voices in songs of triumph, as God the Father
places upon His brow the crown of victory. What a glorious coronation! What a supreme triumph! What an un-
paralleled victory! Oh, Jesus, thou art the monarch of the
skies, thou art king of heaven and earth!

GEORGE LIVINGSTONE ROBINSON

HIS PROMISES

BE WATCHFUL

1 THESSALONIANS 5:2 NRSV
*For you yourselves know very well that the day
of the Lord will come like a thief in the night.*

Although the second coming will be preceded by several signs—the desolating sacrilege (Matthew 24:15), great tribulation (v. 21), darkening of the sun (v. 29), they will not indicate the exact time of Jesus' return. Consequently, there will be many for whom his return will be quite unexpected. It will be as in the days of Noah (Matthew 24:37). Although Noah spent some time in the construction of the ark, none of his contemporaries, except for his own family, prepared themselves for the flood. People will be feeling secure, but sudden destruction will come upon them (1 Thessalonians 5:2–3). Jesus' teachings suggest that because of a long delay before the second coming, some will be lulled into inattention (Matthew 25:1–13; 2 Peter 3:3–4). When the Parousia finally occurs, however, it will happen so quickly that there will be no time to prepare (Matthew 25:8–10). As Louis Berkhof puts it, "The Bible intimates that the measure of surprise at the second coming of Christ will be in an inverse ratio to the measure of their watchfulness."

MILLARD J. ERICKSON

THE GREAT SALVATION

HEBREWS 2:3 NIV
How shall we escape if we ignore such a great salvation?

Suppose I am dying with consumption, which I inherited from my father or mother. . . . Well, I go to my
physician, and to the best physicians, and they all give me
up. They say I am incurable. . . . Well, a friend happens to
come along and looks at me and says: ". . . Ten years ago
I was far gone. I was given up by the physicians to die, but
I took this medicine and it cured me. I am perfectly
well—look at me." . . . He then hands me the medicine.
I dash it to the ground; I do not believe in its saving
power: I die. The reason is, then, that I spurned the
remedy.

So it will not be because Adam fell, but that you spurn
the remedy offered to you to save you. You will have
darkness rather than light. How, then, shall ye escape if ye
neglect so great Salvation? There is no hope for you if you
neglect the remedy.

DWIGHT L. MOODY

OUR AWESOME GOD

LUKE 12:5 NIV
"But I will show you whom you should fear:
Fear him who, after the killing of the body, has power
to throw you into hell. Yes, I tell you, fear him."

He is not only able to cast wicked men into hell, but he can most *easily* do it. Sometimes an earthly prince meets with a great deal of difficulty to subdue a rebel that has found means to fortify himself and has made himself strong by the numbers of his followers. But it is not so with God. There is no fortress that is any defense from the power of God. Though hand join in hand, and vast multitudes of God's enemies combine and associate themselves, they are easily broken in pieces. . . . We find it easy to tread on and crush a worm that we see crawling on the earth; so 'tis easy for us to cut or singe a slender thread that anything hangs by; thus easy is it for God when he pleases to cast his enemies down to hell. What are we that we should think to stand before him at whose rebuke the earth trembles and before whom the rocks are thrown down?

JONATHAN EDWARDS

RULING WITH THE KING

REVELATION 2:26–27 NIV
"To him who overcomes and does my will to the end,
I will give authority over the nations—
'He will rule them with an iron scepter;
he will dash them to pieces like pottery'—
just as I have received authority from my Father."

Christ promises the overcomer that he will rule the nations with a rod of iron. The verb means "to shepherd" and should be taken in the sense of wielding the shepherd's staff or club (the "rod of iron" may have been an oak club capped with iron) to ward off the attacks of marauding beasts. In Revelation 12:5 and 19:15 the prerogative of ruling (shepherding) the nations belongs to the conquering Christ. A share in this rule is promised to the overcomers in Thyatira. The description of this rule as the shattering of the potter's vessel speaks of the absolute power of the victorious Christ and his followers over the rebellious nations. The concluding clause of the verse picks up from verse 26. Christ will give authority to the overcomer as he has received it from his Father. It reflects the messianic "You are my son, today I have begotten you" of Psalm 2:7.

ROBERT H. MOUNCE

THE CONQUERING LORD

REVELATION 1:17 NASB
When I saw Him, I fell at His feet as a dead man.
And He placed His right hand on me, saying,
"Do not be afraid; I am the first and the last . . ."

It is inconceivable that the last public view the world would have of Jesus Christ would be that of a bleeding, dying, crucified criminal, covered with blood, spit, and flies, hanging naked in the Jerusalem twilight. Did you realize that after His resurrection, He never appeared in a public venue before unbelievers? Plenty of believers saw Him, touched Him, spoke to Him, and gave unanimous testimony that He was risen from the dead. But there is no record that unbelievers ever saw Him.

But the unbelieving world will see His glory displayed to everyone. Scripture says, "Christ also, having been offered once to bear the sins of many, will appear a second time for salvation without reference to sin, to those who eagerly await Him" (Hebrews 9:28). The Savior who was humiliated, taunted, and put to death in a public display of humanity's hatred of God will return as conquering Lord in view of the entire world. And every eye will see Him (Revelation 1:7).

JOHN MACARTHUR

Made Alive

1 Corinthians 15:22 ESV
*For as in Adam all die,
so also in Christ shall all be made alive.*

From these words it is argued, that as all mankind died in Adam, so all mankind will live eternally in and through Christ. In this chapter, the apostle is discoursing of the resurrection of Christ's people, the whole body of his followers, verse 23, "But every man in his own order, Christ the first fruits, afterward *they that are Christ's,* at his coming." These words immediately follow those now under consideration, and plainly show the sense of the apostle in the twenty-second verse to be, that all *Christ's,* all his *disciples,* or his *followers* shall be made alive in him. But who those are whom the apostle calls *Christ's,* or his *people,* his *followers,* is not determined in this text. It is however abundantly determined by the whole New Testament, that they are the *penitent* and *believing,* and they only. As all who were in Adam, or were represented by him, died in him; so all who are in Christ, or are represented by him, shall live in him.

Jonathan Edwards

The Climax of History

ACTS 1:11 NIV

"Men of Galilee," they said, "why do you stand here looking into the sky? This same Jesus, who has been taken from you into heaven, will come back in the same way you have seen him go into heaven."

At His ascension, angels appeared to the disciples and gave the promise: "And as they were gazing intently into the sky while He was departing, behold, two men in white clothing stood beside them; and they also said, 'Men of Galilee, why do you stand looking into the sky? This Jesus, who has been taken up from you into heaven, will come in just the same way as you have watched Him go into heaven'" (Acts 1:10–11). Billy Graham obviously takes this word literally. On many occasions he has made his position clear. In a sermon preached in 1962 entitled "Three Keys to Youthfulness," he stressed evangelist D. L. Moody's pronouncement that the world was soon coming to an end; and then he went on to say, "If the world seemed about to come to an end in Moody's time, how much closer must we be to the climax of history?" The climax of history for both Moody and Graham centers in the second coming of Jesus Christ.

LEWIS DRUMMOND

THE LORD OF ALL

MATTHEW 24:30 NIV

*"At that time the sign of the Son of Man will appear
in the sky, and all the nations of the earth will mourn.
They will see the Son of Man coming on the
clouds of the sky, with power and great glory."*

Various descriptions of the return of Christ indicate
its glorious character, a sharp contrast to the lowly
and humble circumstances of his first coming. The latter
was the first stage of Christ's humiliation; the former will
be the final stage of his exaltation. He will come on the
clouds with great power and great glory (Matthew 24:30;
Mark 13:26; Luke 21:27). He will be accompanied by his
angels and heralded by the archangel (1 Thessalonians
4:16). He will sit upon his glorious throne and judge all
the nations (Matthew 25:31–46). The irony of this situation is that he who was judged at the end of his stay on
earth will be the judge over all at his second coming.
Clearly, he will be the triumphant, glorious Lord of all.

MILLARD J. ERICKSON

CHRIST OUR HOPE

*To whom God would make known what is the riches
of the glory of this mystery among the Gentiles;
which is Christ in you, the hope of glory.*

Do you possess this kind of hope? Do you feel that you have to cram all of your expectations and aspirations into the present, or that you have an eternal hope in Christ? Does your hope end at the grave, or does it extend beyond it into eternity? Is your hope in God, and especially in the death and resurrection of Jesus Christ, or is it in material things or in your own efforts?

In this age of despair, there is but one solution: Jesus Christ. He is the One who has provided the forgiveness of sins, and the hope of eternal life. He is the One who will return to this earth, to judge the wicked and to eternally bless His own. His is the only hope which God offers to a sinful, fallen world, a world without hope.

Have you trusted in Him? Is He your hope? That is the message of the gospel. And this is the believer's confidence and joy. May God give you an assurance of this hope, as you trust in Jesus Christ alone.

BOB DEFFINBAUGH

CITIZENS OF HEAVEN

PHILIPPIANS 3:20–21 ESV

*But our citizenship is in heaven, and from it we await
a Savior, the Lord Jesus Christ, who will transform our
lowly body to be like his glorious body, by the power
that enables him even to subject all things to himself.*

Is your citizenship in heaven? Have you laid down the
arms of unbelief and rebellion against Christ? Have you
received the blood-bought amnesty that he offers to all
rebels? Have you bowed the knee of submission and loyalty to the king of the universe? Do it today. And join the
citizens of heaven in "awaiting a Savior, the Lord Jesus
Christ, who will transform our lowly body to be like his
glorious body, by the power that enables him even to subject all things to himself."

JOHN PIPER

GLORIFY GOD WITH YOUR BODIES

PHILIPPIANS 3:20–21 NLT

*But we are citizens of heaven, where the Lord Jesus
Christ lives. And we are eagerly waiting for him to
return as our Savior. He will take these weak mortal
bodies of ours and change them into glorious bodies
like his own, using the same mighty power that
he will use to conquer everything, everywhere.*

I can hear someone say, "Why bother!" Let it go. Who
needs it. All that matters is the spiritual realities of love
and joy and peace and righteousness and goodness and
truth. Why the big fuss over arms and legs and hands and
feet and hair and eyes and ears and tongues? It seems so
earthly. . . .

God did not create the physical universe willy-nilly. He
had a reason, namely, to add to the ways his glory is exter-
nalized and made manifest. "The skies are telling the
glory of God." That's why he made them.

Why does God go to all the trouble to dirty his hands
to reestablish your body and clothe it with immortality?
Because his Son paid the price of his life so that God
could be glorified in your body for ever and ever. "You
were bought with a price, therefore glorify God with
your bodies." God will not dishonor the work of his Son.
That's why he will raise your body.

JOHN PIPER

THE LAMB

LUKE 1:32 NRSV
*"He will be great, and will be called the
Son of the Most High, and the Lord God will
give to him the throne of his ancestor David."*

Christian, here is joy for thee; thou hast looked, and
thou hast seen the Lamb. Through thy tearful eyes
thou hast seen the Lamb taking away thy sins. Rejoice,
then! In a little while, when thine eyes shall have been
wiped from tears, thou wilt see the same Lamb exalted on
his throne. . . . Thou shalt enjoy the constant vision of his
presence, and thou shalt dwell with him. . . . Why, that
Lamb is heaven itself; for as good Rutherford says,
"Heaven and Christ are the same things; to be with Christ
is to be in heaven, and to be in heaven is to be with
Christ." And he very sweetly says in one of his letters,
wrapped up in love to Christ, "Oh! my Lord Christ, if I
could be in heaven without thee, it would be a hell; and
if I could be in hell, and have thee still, it would be a
heaven to me, for thou art all the heaven I want." It is
true, is it not Christian? Does not thy soul say so?

C. H. SPURGEON

WE WILL SEE HIS GLORY

I CORINTHIANS 13:12 NLT

*Now we see things imperfectly as in a poor mirror, but
then we will see everything with perfect clarity. All that
I know now is partial and incomplete, but then I will
know everything completely, just as God knows me now.*

Christ himself, in his own person, with all his glory,
shall be continually with us, before us, proposed
unto us. We shall no longer have an image, a representation of him, such as is the delineation of his glory in the
Gospel. We "shall see him," saith the apostle, "face to
face" (1 Corinthians 13:12); which he opposeth unto our
seeing him darkly as in a glass, which is the utmost that
faith can attain to. "We shall see him as he is" (1 John
3:2)—not as now, in an imperfect description of him. As
a man sees his neighbour when they stand and converse
together face to face, so shall we see the Lord Christ in
his glory. . . .

This I know, that in the immediate beholding of the
person of Christ, we shall see a glory in it a thousand
times above what here we can conceive. The excellencies
of infinite wisdom, love, and power therein, will be continually before us. And all the glories of the person of
Christ which we have before weakly and faintly inquired
into, will be in our sight for evermore.

JOHN OWEN

INEXPRESSIBLE JOY

1 PETER 1:8–9 NIV

Though you have not seen him, you love him;
and even though you do not see him now,
you believe in him and are filled with an
inexpressible and glorious joy, for you are receiving
the goal of your faith, the salvation of your souls.

Augustus Toplady, who wrote "Rock of Ages," died in London at the age of 38. When death drew near he said, "It is my dying vow that these great and glorious truths which the Lord in rich mercy has given me to believe and enabled me to preach are now brought into practical and heartfelt experience. They are the very joy and support of my soul. The comfort flowing from them carries me far above the things of time and sin." Then he said, "Had I wings like a dove I would fly away to the bosom of God and be at rest." About an hour before he died he seemed to awaken from a gentle slumber, and his last words were, "Oh! What delight! Who can fathom the joys of heaven! I know it cannot be long now until my Savior will come for me." And then bursting into a flood of tears he said, "All is light, light, light, light, the brightness of His own glory. Oh come Lord Jesus, come, come quickly!" And he closed his eyes.

JOHN MACARTHUR

ABOUT HEAVEN

And I heard a loud voice from the throne saying, "Now the dwelling of God is with men, and he will live with them. They will be his people, and God himself will be with them and be their God."

REVELATION 21:3 NIV

ABOUT HEAVEN

If the gospel accounts are any indication, Jesus had the kingdom of heaven constantly on His mind—as a true king would. One of the startling aspects of Jesus' kingdom is the way He offers citizenship to those who wouldn't be allowed in the door anywhere else. Meanwhile, those who consider themselves eminently qualified get turned away at the gate. The management of the kingdom is offensive to some and good news to others. But Jesus, as the King, sets the standard and makes the commitments.

His promises are royal decrees. As you read about them in the pages to come, think about the privilege you have to be a citizen of His kingdom. How does that honor affect the way you live your life?

THE HOME OF THE REDEEMED

1 CORINTHIANS 2:9 NKJV

*But as it is written: "Eye has not seen, nor ear heard,
Nor have entered into the heart of man The things
which God has prepared for those who love Him."*

Heaven! A comforting word is this! But who among us mortal creatures can envision its blessed reality? Neither the artist's brush, the sculptor's chisel, nor the theologian's exegesis can depict the things which God hath prepared for them who love Him. The wonder, the glory, and the effulgence of the home of the redeemed will be seen only through the eyes of our glorified bodies when we awake in Christ's likeness. "Now we see through a glass, darkly; but then face to face: now I know in part; but then shall I know even as also I am known" (1 Corinthians 13:12). Still we are not left alone to grope in dark ignorance. A foretaste of glory divine has been preserved for us upon the pages of God's eternal and unerring Word.

LEHMAN STRAUSS

AT HOME WITH GOD

JOHN 14:2 NIV
"In my Father's house are many rooms;
if it were not so, I would have told you.
I am going there to prepare a place for you."

This of itself is enough to give us hopeful thoughts of the future state. Christ is busied in preparing for us what will give us satisfaction and joy. When we expect a guest we love and have written for, we take pleasure in preparing for his reception—we hang in his room the picture he likes; if he is infirm, we wheel in the easiest chair; we gather the flowers he admires and set them on his table; we go back and back to see if nothing else will suggest itself to us so that when he comes he may have entire satisfaction. This is enough for us to know—that Christ is similarly occupied. He knows our tastes, our capabilities, our attainments, and he has identified a place as ours and holds it for us. What the joys and the activities and occupations of the future shall be we do not know. . . . But we do know that at home with God the fullest life that man can live will certainly be ours.

MARCUS DODS

FIX YOUR EYES ON THE KINGDOM

HEBREWS 11:8-10 NIV

*By faith Abraham, when called to go to a place he
would later receive as his inheritance, obeyed and went,
even though he did not know where he was going.
By faith he made his home in the promised land like
a stranger in a foreign country; he lived in tents, . . .
For he was looking forward to the city with foundations,
whose architect and builder is God.*

I heard a man, some time ago, speaking about Abraham.
He said "Abraham was not tempted by the well-
watered plains of Sodom, for Abraham was what you
might call a long-sighted man; he had his eyes set on the
city which had foundation—whose Builder and Maker is
God." But Lot was a short-sighted man; and there are
many people in the Church who are very short-sighted;
they only see things right around them they think
good. . . . They want one eye for the world and the other
for the Kingdom of God. . . . When the Spirit of God is
on us we will just let go the things of time and lay hold
of things eternal. This is Church's need today; we want
the Spirit to come in mighty power and consume all the
vile dross there is in us. Oh! that the Spirit of fire may
come down and burn everything in us that is contrary to
God's blessed Word and Will.

DWIGHT L. MOODY

PARADISE

PHILIPPIANS 3:20 NIV
*But our citizenship is in heaven. And we eagerly
await a Savior from there, the Lord Jesus Christ.*

Always remember that we have renounced the world
and are living here as guests and strangers in the
meantime. Anticipate the day assigned to each of us for
our homecoming. This day will snatch us up, set us free
from the snares of the world, and return us to Paradise and
the kingdom. Who, in foreign lands, wouldn't hurry to
return to their own country? Who, when rushing to
return to his friends, wouldn't eagerly want the winds at
his back so that he could embrace those dear to him
sooner? We consider paradise as our country. . . . A great
number of our dear ones are waiting for us there. . . . Let
us long to be with them and to come to Christ quickly.
May God see our eager desire. May the Lord Jesus Christ
look at the purpose of our mind and faith. He will give
the larger rewards of His glory to those with a greater
desire for Him!

CYPRIAN

THE DEATH OF THE RIGHTEOUS

1 CORINTHIANS 15:54 NLT

When this happens—when our perishable earthly bodies have been transformed into heavenly bodies that will never die—then at last the Scriptures will come true: "Death is swallowed up in victory."

There is, indeed, a vast difference between the death of the righteous and that of the wicked. To the latter, death is the effect of the law-curse, and the harbinger of everlasting destruction; but to the former, death is not the proper punishment of sin, but the termination of all sin and sorrow, and an entrance into life eternal. To them death is divested of its sting and rendered powerless to do them any real injury. Not only is it disarmed of its power to hurt them—it is compelled to perform a friendly part to them. It is their release from warfare—their deliverance from woe—their departure to be with Christ. But although death is no real loss but rather great gain to the righteous, yet, as it consists in the dissolution of the union between the soul and the body, it is an event from which they are not exempted.

ROBERT SHAW

TRUE FREEDOM

2 PETER 3:13 NIV

But in keeping with his promise we are looking forward to a new heaven and a new earth, the home of righteousness.

The days of this life are short and evil, full of sorrow and misery, where a person is stained with many sins, ensnared by many passions, bound by many fears, swollen by many cares, distracted by many curiosities, entangled by many vanities, surrounded by many mistakes, weakened by many efforts, weighed down by temptations, sapped by pleasures, tormented by want.

Oh, when will there be an end to all these things that have gone awry in God's plan? When shall I be freed from the wretched slavery of my sins? When shall I be mindful, Lord, of you alone? When shall I fully rejoice in you? When shall I be truly free, without anything standing in my way, with no inner confusion and conflict? When shall I find a solid peace—peace calm and secure, peace inside and out, peace firm in every way? . . . Oh, when shall I be with you in your kingdom, which you have prepared for your beloved from all eternity?

THOMAS À KEMPIS

HEAVEN ON EARTH

PSALM 16:11 ESV
You make known to me the path of life;
in your presence there is fullness of joy;
at your right hand are pleasures forevermore.

Heaven consists in nothing else than walking, abiding, resting in the Divine Presence. There are souls who enter into this heaven before leaving the body. If thou believest that thy God, found, felt, and rested in, is heaven, why not, under the gracious help which He vouchsafes to thee in His Son, *begin at once to discipline and qualify thy soul for this heaven?* If this be thy chief good, why turn away from it, as though it were a thing not to be desired? If it be the very end of thy being, the only right, good, and blessed end, why postpone thy qualification for it, as though it were a bitter necessity? Suffer thy soul, so noble in its origin, to be withdrawn from dust, noise, multitudes, vain treasures, and vain pleasures, to find its sweetness and fulness in God.

JOHN PULSFORD

Unhindered Enjoyment

REVELATION 5:5–6 ESV

And one of the elders said to me, "Weep no more;
behold, the Lion of the tribe of Judah,
the Root of David, has conquered . . ."
And between the throne and the four living creatures
and among the elders I saw a Lamb standing,
as though it had been slain.

When the saints shall see Christ's glory and exaltation in heaven, it will . . . serve only to heighten
their surprise and joy, when they find Christ condescend-
ing to admit them to such intimate access and so freely
and fully communicating himself to them. So that if we
choose Christ for our friend and portion, we shall hereafter be so received to him, that there shall be nothing to
hinder the fullest enjoyment of him, to the satisfying the
utmost cravings of our souls. We may take our full swing
at gratifying our spiritual appetite after these holy pleasures. Christ will then say, as in Song [of Songs] 5:1, "Eat,
O friends, drink, yea, drink abundantly O beloved." And
this shall be our entertainment to all eternity! There shall
never be any end of this happiness, or anything to inter-
rupt our enjoyment of it, or in the least to molest us in it!

JONATHAN EDWARDS

SEEING THE FACE OF GOD

REVELATION 22:4 NLT
And they will see his face,
and his name will be written on their foreheads.

When John speaks of the blessings of the heavenly city, the culmination of those blessings comes in the short statement, *"They shall see his face"* (22:4). When we look into the face of our Lord and he looks back at us with infinite love, we will see in him the fulfillment of everything that we know to be good and right and desirable in the universe. . . . As we gaze into the face of our Lord, we will know more fully than ever before that "in your presence there is fullness of joy, at your right hand are pleasures for evermore" (Psalm 16:11). Then will be fulfilled the longing of our hearts with which we have cried out in the past, "One thing I have asked of the Lord, that will I seek after; that I may dwell in the house of the Lord all the days of my life, *to behold the beauty of the Lord*, and to inquire in his temple" (Psalm 27:4).

WAYNE GRUDEM

COME TO CHRIST

JOHN 14:2–3 NKJV

"In My Father's house are many mansions; if it were not so, I would have told you. I go to prepare a place for you. And if I go and prepare a place for you, I will come again and receive you to Myself; that where I am, there you may be also."

There is mercy enough in God to admit an innumerable multitude into heaven. There is mercy enough for all, and there is merit enough in Christ to purchase heavenly happiness for millions of millions. . . .

There are sufficient and suitable accommodations for all the different sorts of persons that are in the world: for great and small, for high and low, rich and poor, wise and unwise, bond and free, persons of all nations and all conditions and circumstances, for those that have been great sinners as well as for moral livers; for weak saints and those that are babes in Christ as well as for those that are stronger and more grown in grace. There is in heaven a sufficiency for the happiness of every sort; there is a convenient accommodation for every creature that will hearken to the calls of the Gospel. None that will come to Christ, let his condition be what it will, need to fear but that Christ will provide a place suitable for him in heaven.

JONATHAN EDWARDS

PERFECT REST

REVELATION 14:13 NRSV
And I heard a voice from heaven saying,
"Write this: Blessed are the dead who from now on
die in the Lord." "Yes," says the Spirit, "they will
rest from their labors, for their deeds follow them."

To my mind, one of the best views of heaven is that *it is a land of rest*—especially to the working man. Those who have not to work hard think they will love heaven as a place of service. That is very true. But to the working man, to the man who toils with his brain or with his hands, it must ever be a sweet thought that there is a land where we shall rest. . . . You will not have to drive the ploughshare into the unthankful soil in heaven, you will not need to rise to daily toils before the sun hath risen and labor still when the sun hath long ago gone to his rest; but ye shall be still, ye shall be quiet, ye shall rest yourselves, for all are rich in heaven, all are happy there, all are peaceful. Toil, trouble, travail, and labor are words that cannot be spelled in heaven; they have no such things there, for they always rest.

C. H. SPURGEON

SWEET ENJOYMENT

I JOHN 2:25 NRSV
And this is what he has promised us, eternal life.

Every wall of separation between them and God is taken down, every cloud which hid his face is dispersed, every frown smoothed into smiles. They are admitted to the perfect vision and sweet enjoyment of God and the Lamb. They see that God does not reproach them for the past, that he has not one less tender feeling towards them for all their sins, and that he loves them with an affection infinitely surpassing that of the tenderest earthly parent. They are conscious of an interchange of thoughts and feelings with him most affectionate, of a communion no less real than that which subsists between earthly friends. They possess greatly enlarged views of his perfections, particularly of his unbounded love, and enjoy him to a degree of which we have here no conception. Their souls swell and expand with the mighty blessedness, and rise into raptures of wonder, love, and praise.

EDWARD GRIFFIN

CHRIST IS OUR HAPPINESS

REVELATION 2:7 NASB

"He who has an ear, let him hear what the Spirit says to the churches. To him who overcomes, I will grant to eat of the tree of life which is in the Paradise of God."

Look to Christ, not only to give you all, but to be your all; for he is not only the way to life, but the life itself: "I am the way, the truth, and the life." "As I desire," says one, "never to be happy, if Christ be not able to bring me to happiness, so I desire no greater, no better happiness, than what Christ is, and can be to me." O sirs, he is all, and there is all in him; all to justify, all to sanctify, all to glorify, all to fill and satisfy, all to delight and solace the largest faculties of the immortal soul; "in his presence there is fulness of joy." The highest happiness here is, "Christ in us the hope of glory" and the highest happiness hereafter is Christ, even to be for ever with the Lord. The thief on the cross had this preached to him, "This day shalt thou be with me in Paradise." To be in Paradise is not happiness; to be with angels there is not happiness; but to be with Christ there, this is heaven and happiness.

RALPH ERSKINE

THE MISSING ELEMENTS OF PARADISE

REVELATION 21:3 NASB
And I heard a loud voice from the throne, saying,
"Behold, the tabernacle of God is among men,
and He will dwell among them, and they shall be
His people, and God Himself will be among them."

Paradise has some missing elements, because God has deliberately omitted certain familiar aspects of earthly life.

First, there will be no churches or sanctuaries. This means I will be out of a job, but I won't mind a bit. Why would there be need for a church, when our cause to worship is present with us?

We will not see the sun, but there will be no cloudy days. His light will be among us forevermore. . . .

We will never be separated from our loved ones. There will be no painful farewells, just a prolonged love story. No arguments, no hurt feelings, no injured egos.

Doctors and dentists will also be out of work, for there will be no sickness and no pain. People who have been confined to wheel chairs will be able to run; the blind will see unmarred beauty; the deaf will hear the heavenly choirs; the wounded will be whole.

DAVID JEREMIAH

ETERNITY WITH GOD

I CORINTHIANS 15:51-53, 58 NIV

Listen, I tell you a mystery: We will not all sleep, but
we will all be changed—in a flash, in the twinkling of
an eye, at the last trumpet. For the trumpet will sound,
the dead will be raised imperishable, and we will be
changed. For the perishable must clothe itself with the
imperishable, and the mortal with immortality. . . .
Therefore, my dear brothers, stand firm. Let
nothing move you. Always give yourselves fully
to the work of the Lord, because you know
that your labor in the Lord is not in vain.

Thus we are ever firmly assured by God's word that after this wretched and fleeting existence, in which we are never safe for even one moment, there shall be an eternal and blessed life and kingdom. Otherwise we would have to blot out the First Commandment along with the entire gospel and Holy Scriptures. What would be the use of a God solely for this fleeting life in which they flourish best who have no God? But if there is a God, as all devout and pious souls firmly and steadfastly believe and in which faith they live and die, then we shall not only live here for a brief time but also eternally in the place where God is.

MARTIN LUTHER

LONG FOR GOD HIMSELF

1 JOHN 3:2–3 NLT

*Yes, dear friends, we are already God's children,
and we can't even imagine what we will be like
when Christ returns. But we do know that when
he comes we will be like him, for we will see him
as he really is. And all who believe this will keep
themselves pure, just as Christ is pure.*

The whole life of a good Christian is a holy desire to
see God as he is. Now what you long for, you do not
yet see, but longing makes you capable of being filled
when at last you behold what you have desired. . . . God,
by making us wait in hope, stretches our desire; by making
us desire, he stretches our soul; by stretching our soul,
he makes it capable of holding more. . . .

This is our life as Christians: to be filled with longing.
But holy desire fills us only to the extent that we cut
off our longings from the love of the world. You must
first empty what you want to be filled. If you are to be
filled with what is good, then you must pour out what is
evil. . . . In truth, we are to be filled with Something
beyond words: God himself. We must stretch ourselves
out to him, then, so that when he comes, he may fill us.

AUGUSTINE

FOLLOW JESUS TO ETERNAL LIFE

MATTHEW 7:21 ESV

"Not everyone who says to me, 'Lord, Lord,'
will enter the kingdom of heaven, but the one who
does the will of my Father who is in heaven."

To many it seems a hard speech, "Deny thyself, take up thy cross, and follow Jesus." But it will be much harder to hear that other word, "Depart from me, ye cursed"; for only they who now hear and follow the word of the cross shall then have no fear of the word of condemnation. For the sign of the cross will be seen in the heaven when the Lord cometh to judgment, and all the servants of the cross, who in their lifetime have been conformed to Christ crucified, will then draw near to Christ their judge with great confidence. Why, then, dost thou fear to take up the cross which fitteth thee for the kingdom? In the cross is life, in the cross is salvation; the cross defends against all enemies; in the cross there is the infusion of all heavenly sweetness. . . . There is no happiness for the soul but in the cross. Take up, therefore, thy cross and follow Jesus, and thou shalt live forever.

ANDREW MURRAY

NEW LIFE

1 CORINTHIANS 15:22-23 NLT

*Everyone dies because all of us are related to Adam,
the first man. But all who are related to Christ, the
other man, will be given new life. But there is an order
to this resurrection: Christ was raised first; then when
Christ comes back, all his people will be raised.*

O Son of God and Son of Man,
Thou wast incarnate, didst suffer, rise, ascend for
my sake;
Thy departure was not a token of separation but a
pledge of return;
Thy Word, promises, sacraments, show thy death until
thou come again. . . .
I have trusted thee and thou hast not betrayed my trust;
waited for thee, and not waited in vain.
Thou wilt come to raise my body from the dust, and
re-unite it to my soul. . . .
And after judgment, peace and rest, life and service,
employment and enjoyment, for thine elect.
O God, keep me in this faith, and ever looking for
Christ's return.

UNKNOWN

NEW BODIES

I CORINTHIANS 15:42–43 ESV
*So is it with the resurrection of the dead. What is
sown is perishable; what is raised is imperishable.
It is sown in dishonor; it is raised in glory.
It is sown in weakness; it is raised in power.*

After the corn is thus dead and buried, then it quick-
eneth and reviveth to life: so also shall it be with our
body; for after it is laid in the grave and buried, it shall
then quicken, rise, and revive.

Again, as to the manner of its change in its rising, this
similitude also doth fitly suit.

It is sown a dead corn; it is raised a living one. It is sown
dry and without comeliness; it riseth green and beautiful.
It is sown a single corn; it riseth a full ear. It is sown in its
husk, but in its rising it leaveth that husk behind it.

Further, though the kernel thus die, be buried, and
meet with all this change and alteration in these things,
yet none of them can cause the nature of the kernel to
cease—it is wheat still. . . . God giveth it a body as it
pleaseth him, "but to every seed his own body."

JOHN BUNYAN

Day 364

LOVING GOD PERFECTLY

1 CORINTHIANS 13:10 NIV
But when perfection comes, the imperfect disappears.

M y God, let me know and love you, so that I may
find my happiness in you. Since I cannot fully
achieve this on earth, help me to improve daily until I
may do so to the full. Enable me to know you ever more
on earth, so that I may know you perfectly in heaven.
Enable me to love you ever more on earth, so that I may
love you perfectly in heaven. In that way my joy may
be great on earth, and perfect with you in heaven.
O God of truth, grant me the happiness of heaven so that
my joy may be full in accord with your promise. In the
meantime let my mind dwell on that happiness, my
tongue speak of it, my heart pine for it, my mouth pronounce it, my soul hunger for it, my flesh thirst for it, and
my entire being desire it until I enter through death in the
joy of my Lord forever. Amen.

AUGUSTINE

UNIMAGINABLE GLORY

1 THESSALONIANS 4:17 NIV
And so we will be with the Lord forever.

If the thought of unending life for trillions and trillions of years is oppressive to you because of the threat of boredom, remember this: though it is not fully comprehensible to us, an infinite God is infinitely inexhaustible in the treasures of power and wisdom and love and beauty which we can spend an eternity discovering and enjoying and applying to daily life in the new earth. We will never sit down like Alexander the Great and weep that there are no more worlds to conquer. Our joyous quest to attain the heights of God's wisdom and love will never be ended. When, after a million years, we pull ourselves with unspeakable exhilaration over the massive peak of some glorious divine truth, we will be utterly astonished to find ourselves not at the top, but merely in the foothills, and before us, as far as the eye can see, mountains and valleys and forests and height and light that we could have never imagined. There will be no boredom in the age to come. O, to be there and not in hell!

JOHN PIPER